"Social Security Income Planning: The Baby Boomers' Guide to Maximize Your Retirement Benefits"

Written By: **Mark J. Orr, CFP®**

Certified Financial Planner™

and fee-based Registered Investment Advisor

Join My Retirement Income Planning "Tips" Email list for more great financial planning and retirement tips. Simply visit my website below and register.

Visit my website: **SmartFinancialPlanning.com**

4th Edition -- Copyright 2016

Preface

On Monday, November 2, 2015, President Obama signed into law the Bipartisan Budget Act of 2015, which includes significant changes to the Social Security advanced claiming strategies that were described in the earlier editions of this book. This latest edition contains the FULLY UPDATED rules regarding Social Security claiming strategies.

Some 10,000 Americans are turning age 62 each and every day. There are few more important decisions that most about-to-retire folks will make than when (and how) to start receiving their Social Security retirement benefits. Many people simply decide to get benefits as soon as they are able – with very little regard for their own (and even their spouses) long term future retirement security.

Making hasty or un-researched Social Security decisions can have serious long-term financial consequences. It is the author's opinion that making decisions about when and how to take your Social Security benefits on a "standalone basis" is a HUGE mistake. Nearly everyone should only make their Social Security benefit choices within the context of their entire retirement plan. Not only must one take into consideration their retirement lifestyle and legacy goals, but also the types and amount of their assets, their tolerance for risk, their life expectancy (their own and their spouse's) and many other factors.

Before making a nearly "unfixable" mistake, learn about all of your Social Security benefit options, savvy filing strategies as well as smart ways to reduce your taxes. Read, learn and enjoy... Mark J. Orr, CFP®

Thank you for purchasing this book.
Up to $1,000 a year of royalties from this book will be donated to The Rotary Foundation

What's Inside This Book

Introduction

The Retirement Income Challenge

Understanding the Lifetime Value of Social Security Benefits

A Brief History of the Social Security Program

How Social Security is Funded and How You Qualify for Benefits?

How Are Your Social Security Benefits Calculated?

Full Retirement Age (FRA) for Social Security

Taking Early Retirement Benefits

Historical Automatic Cost-Of-Living Adjustments

Delaying Starting Your Social Security Benefits

How Does the "Earnings Test" Work

Spousal Benefits Introduction

Life Expectancy Table – How Long Might You Live

Much More on Spousal Benefits

Social Security Benefits for Divorced Spouses

How Do Survivor's Benefits Work?

The Taxation of Your Social Security Benefits

Two Potential Social Security Gotchas (WEP & GPO)!

Social Security Strategies to Maximize Lifetime Income

The "REAL WORLD" Filing "Breakeven" Analysis

Investing Your Monthly Social Security Checks

File and Suspend – Learn What 98% of Retirees Miss Out On

Get Some Income Now... Get MORE Later – A Powerful Strategy

The Proven 62/70 Strategy

Some Savvy Income Tax Planning Strategies – the story of
        the Earlys, the Waites and the Bests

Social Security Planning for Retirees with Minor Children

Social Security and Medicare

How Secure is Social Security?

How Secure is Your Pension from an Employer?

The 3 Buckets of Risk and the 3 Buckets of Taxation

Putting Retirement ALL Together

Final Thoughts About Filing for Your Social Security Benefits

"Social Security Income Planning: The Baby Boomers' Guide to Maximize Your Retirement Benefits"

Introduction

On November 2, 2015 President Obama signed the Bi-Partisan Budget Bill. The stated primary purpose of this bill was to increase the Federal debt limit -- so the Social Security rules have changed!

In this Bill, Congress included Section 831 titled "Closure of Unintended Loopholes" which effectively phased out two powerful Social Security claiming strategies – "File and Suspend" and filing a "Restricted Application". This bill made the single largest change to Social Security since the Citizens Freedom to Work Act of 2000, which first enabled both of these savvy filing strategies.

In earlier editions of this book, I asked "why in the world do we need another book on how to choose the best way to claim your Social Security benefits in order to maximize your retirement income"? Although the rules have now changed, this is still one of the most important retirement income decisions that you need to make!

There are dozens of books on this timely subject that have been written for people who are about to decide how and when to take their Social Security benefits. Most of them are now "outdated" with the new rules. Before this change, I'd bought and read about 6-7 of the best-selling ones on this subject and most all of them were very good. A few were written more for financial advisers and might be "overkill" for the average reader, while one was so basic as to be of little retirement planning value. But in my opinion, one important thing or another was missing from each and every one of them.

Let me ask you something. How many times does the average person "retire"? Just one time! There really aren't any mulligans or do-overs (except once within your first 12 months of collecting your Social Security checks if you pay them every penny back). Do you really want to "wing it" or make a filing decision based on what your neighbors or co-workers suggest?

There are no "right" or "wrong" claiming decisions or rules of thumb that fit the "average" person. And even if there were... are YOU an average person or couple? If you can get a clear understanding of how it all works and the pros and cons of your many claiming choices, at least you can make the best decision for your personal financial circumstances and retirement goals. But making a poor choice due to ignorance is the last thing that anyone should want to do.

Social Security is complicated. There is not a book out there (at least none that anyone would take a hundred hours to wade through) that will provide the answers to every single question or describe every possible unique circumstance that a single or divorced person, a widow(er) or married couple might find themselves in. Nor should there be! No publication could do that (or do it well). But a great book on this subject can be invaluable to you and is well worth the investment of about ten bucks and some time to read it.

Articles in magazines, a short chapter in a general book on retirement planning or generic online Social Security calculators are just that – one-dimensional sets of information or basic math calculators. **You should also know that employees of the Social Security Administration are not equipped, trained or even allowed to help you make your filing decisions. They are not permitted to give you any guidance or assistance and they cannot offer any recommendations or advice to you.** At the end of the day, it's all up to you to make your best guess or get professional help.

With so much at stake, more and more people look for a financial planner who is well educated on Social Security -- someone who owns and uses powerful Social Security income planning software that can provide them with easy-to-understand explanations of their hundreds of filing alternatives. An advisor who actually specializes in "retirement income planning" to help them coordinate Social Security with their other retirement income resources in order to cover any potential income gaps to help ensure they enjoy a long and prosperous retirement.

So although there is not any book that will replace that personal service, I wrote this book for soon-to-be retirees who want to not only fully understand their filing options, but to totally grasp their choices within the context of their "overall retirement income plan". I want my readers to have more than enough knowledge to ask the right questions and be able to discuss this subject intelligently. I want you to know enough that you don't make a disastrous mistake out of ignorance. I want you to realize the benefits and many financial ramifications of whatever filing choices you make.

One of those ramifications is income taxes. To my knowledge, there is not another book that is written for consumers that has a story like the Earlys, the Waites and the Bests where the reader learns how it is very possible to cut one's taxable income and their subsequent retirement income tax bill by up to 50%. Many savvy readers can learn how to save $1,000's of income tax dollars every year during their retirement – without reducing their actual monthly income. The I.R.S. hopes that you don't learn about and take advantage of these simple rules. And most CPAs will never show you this either.

Now if, for whatever reason, you have not saved (or kept) any money for retirement, have little or no ability or desire to work any longer than you have to and Social Security will be 90% or more of your monthly income for the rest of your life, then none of the good books on this subject will be of much value to you. My best basic advice to you if you believe you (or your spouse) will live a long life is to keep working for as long as possible and delay your Social Security benefits for as long as you can. If your current health condition will likely shorten your lifespan, take your benefits as soon as you can.

But for the other half of Americans who have saved a nice nest-egg, you likely have more flexibility and control in your Social Security decision making process. This book is for you. Getting the "most possible lifetime" dollars from Social Security is likely a significant objective of yours. Saving taxes in retirement is likely a worthy ambition. Nobody wants to pay more taxes than they have to. Perhaps leaving a legacy might be another goal.

The chapter about the 3 buckets of investment risk and the 3 taxation buckets is the perfect complement to learning about filing strategies since Social Security was never, ever meant to provide for 100% of a retirees income. Not only is this discussion vital for soon-to-be retirees, it should be required reading for every American adult before they EVER invest a single dollar anywhere.

On November 4, 2015, I was quoted and this book was cited in the USA Today in an article about the new laws: "The decision on how and when to file for Social Security should be made as part of an overall retirement income plan with your financial goals, life expectancies and financial fears firmly in mind". It's my goal for both middle class and affluent baby boomers to realize that. Your filing decisions should fit within your overall retirement plan so you can have enough income from investments, pensions or any other sources to allow you to have the retirement lifestyle that you want – for as long as you live. It's all about enjoying a retirement lifestyle that should not be adversely affected by recessions, bear markets or even pro-longed periods of low interest rates like we've seen for the last five years.

Although you cannot get your lifetime benefits in a lump sum, leave it to your children and you must play by Social Security's rules, it's your money and is a very important retirement resource. You funded it through your payroll deductions for decades. I hope that you treat it like the big and important decision that it is.

So I promise that by reading this book, you will feel much more confident in making the "best" Social Security filing decision. Whether you make that choice with or without professional help, it's a one-time decision that should absolutely be based on your own unique personal circumstances and retirement goals. So let's get started, OK?

The Retirement Income Challenge

According to the Pew Research Center, some 3,600,000 baby boomers are turning age 62 every year! And almost every one of them will have to make a decision on whether to apply for Social Security benefits right away, or delay making their application for just a few years... or up until they turn age 70. In financial terms, there's a lot "riding" on the decisions each of us will make.

The Wharton School's Pension Research Council recently conducted an important study that shows how pretty low America's Social Security "literacy" rate is. While 70% of those people surveyed said they felt "somewhat" or "very knowledgeable" about Social Security... less than 20% actually scored well on a test to gauge their real literacy on the vital subject of Social Security.

That's a pretty large "disconnect" for something so important as understanding Social Security. Considering that the Social Security Handbook has more than 2,700 separate rules governing its benefits, it's not a surprise that more and more soon-to-retire Americans are looking for professional financial advisers who can help them navigate the program's many intricacies to fully optimize their potential lifetime benefits within the context of their overall financial circumstances.

For 95% of Americans, no matter where you are on the financial spectrum as you near retirement, Social Security will likely play a large role in your retirement by providing a monthly income that you cannot outlive. Not only will it provide an income that can be counted on for the rest of your life – irrespective of the economy, the stock, bond or real estate markets, but an income that should rise along with inflation over the decades to come.

Hopefully you will have more financial resources available to you other than just the monthly Social Security check since the program was never meant to provide for all of your income during your so-called golden years.

In their 23rd Employee Benefit Research Institute on retirement confidence, the institute reports that a disheartening 60% of American workers have a total of under $25,000 in savings and investments (exclusive of pensions and the value of their home). Just 14% of those surveyed claimed that they were confident they would be able to retire comfortably – and based on my professional experience I agree with that figure. That's about the percentage who will be able to live in a similar lifestyle during their retirement as they did while working.

About half of all American retirees get more than 50% of their retirement income from Social Security. It's likely that these folks have been the "working poor" during their careers, so their monthly Social Security benefit check is likely to be pretty low since it is based on their low contributions (corresponding to their low lifetime wages). Others in this group who will heavily rely on Social Security are those who made a good living... but for one reason or another, have no savings to speak of.

Again, on the opposite end of the annual income spectrum, for those who had low annual earnings throughout their working career, Social Security should "replace" about 54% of their past income. That means that they will need to replace some 46% of their past income from other sources (IRA, 401(K), 403(b) distributions, pensions, etc.) or from continuing to work on a full or part time basis for the rest of their lives. Most of these folks will have to keep working.

For fewer and fewer Americans, other sources of retirement income will include a company or government pension. For many more retirees, it will be the potential of drawing income from IRA's, 401(k)'s or other qualified retirement plans.

For the wealthy, (the top 4%-6%), Social Security will not play a meaningful role in securing a comfortable retirement. Those fortunate folks, who have earned a lifetime of maximum countable earnings (currently $118,500 in 2016), will see Social Security "replace" just 27% or much less of that earned income level. Hopefully, those who have made $200,000 annually or more during their working career have substantial savings to depend upon to continue their lifestyle, since they will see a much lower benefit in terms of the amount of earned income that monthly Social Security checks will replace.

To summarize, for most American retirees, Social Security will only "replace" somewhere between 27% and 54% of their earned income during their retirement years. Of course, all of those replacement ratios assume that retirees will need the same income during their retirement years as they did during their working years.

For many retirees, their expenses will go down substantially. For example if their mortgage just got paid off or they downsized their living accommodations. Perhaps you will move to a state with lower costs of living including lower state income and real estate taxes. Of course you will not be making any further contributions 401(K) plan, IRA, etc. nor have any career-related expenses at that point.

However, with more leisure time, a new retiree may spend more money on travel, hobbies (more rounds of golf, fishing trips) and "uncovered" general health care costs and eventually perhaps long-term care (LTC) costs at home or in some type of senior facility.

The bottom line for all but the very wealthy, is that the monthly Social Security check(s) will play a major or very important role during one's retirement years. And even for the wealthy, the monthly Social Security check -- with potential cost of living adjustments (COLAs) included, could easily add up to nearly $1.4 million dollars over a 30+ year retirement. That is nothing to sneeze at no matter how much someone has accumulated during their working career.

The Lifetime Value of Social Security Benefits

As just discussed, for most American retirees, Social Security will represent a very important income stream (which should rise with inflation) that they cannot outlive. Making the correct choices on when and how to file for benefits will have a lasting financial impact for the rest of their life as well as the life of their spouse.

That's right, the lifetime value of those monthly Social Security checks is much larger than most folks realize. For example, under the benefit formula that is currently in place, a retiree who starts receiving the maximum monthly benefit of $2,639 in 2016 (less than the $2,663 in 2015) will enjoy a total of more than $385,000 if he/she lives just 10 years, over $850,000 if he/she lives 20 years and a whopping $1.4 million over 30 years (all figures include an assumed COLA of 2.8%).

Here is another example of the lifetime value of your benefits and the importance of cost of living adjustments (COLA's). Like many of my readers, if your monthly Social Security benefit today is $2,000 and you (or your surviving spouse) live:

10 more years	You (or perhaps your surviving spouse) will receive approximately:	$304,000	Over your lifetime of benefits assuming COLA's @ 2.8% annually
20 more years		$673,000	
30 more years		$1,160,000	

All of those lifetime benefit figures could be much larger – or much smaller based on the decisions one makes when choosing to begin benefits. Making these decisions without knowing how long one will live (or their spouse), potential rates of returns of other investments, future inflation rates, taxation issues, etc. is not easy.

Something the last generation of retirees probably never asked their financial advisor, is how it is possible to maximize their benefits? They simply retired when they felt they could (or were forced to).

The results from a recent survey show that nearly 68% of people feel that their financial advisor should be able to help them make the right decisions regarding Social Security benefits. That would seem reasonable, doesn't it?

But the fact is only 7% or so of the nation's million plus CPAs, investment advisers, stockbrokers, and insurance agents have had any serious training, have extensive experience or even have the necessary software tools to truly help people in this regard. Nor do most of them have the overall experience or are very proficient with the financial tools to help people make the filing decision they ultimately feel they should make. That will become clearer by the end of the book.

Before the 2000-2002 and 2008/2009 recessions, I would say that many advisers didn't even add in (or count) the monthly income benefits of Social Security – as stocks were in a multi-year bull market and some even doubted the long-term existence of the program.

There is absolutely nothing wrong with using the current Social Security rules to your full advantage. As we go forward in this book, you will read about a number of ways you can maximize your Social Security benefits simply by knowing the rules and making smarter decisions.

There are no right or wrong answers or rules of thumb that work for everyone. Each individual's circumstances are different and before making ANY decisions on benefits, your entire financial picture should be looked at carefully from all angles and fully coordinated with the entirety of one's full financial situation and personal goals. Again, your Social Security filing decisions should be based on all factors which will affect your retirement... and not be made in a vacuum.

This is even more critical when one is married, since the highest lifetime wage earner's decisions will impact both of them for as long as either of them live.

Before we go further, we should probably look at a quick history of Social Security so the reader will get a much clearer sense of the program to better understand where we are and where the program will likely go. It's also pretty interesting information.

A Brief History of the Social Security Program

As you will see, from the very beginning, this social program has gone through many changes. There is absolutely no doubt that there will be many more changes to come (as we did November 2, 2015), Some may be pretty easy to make a guess about while others may be less so. The law change in late 2015 quickly came out of nowhere.

Social Security was created by the United States Congress with the Social Security Act of 1935. According to Edward Berkowitz (a professor of both history and public policy at George Washington University), and a leading authority on the history of the Social Security program, it was due to the harsh economic conditions at the time (in the aftermath of the Great Depression) which led President Franklin Roosevelt to envision and create the program.

Berkowitz emphasized that Roosevelt never intended that the Social Security program (paid out as a lump sum back then rather than monthly) as a "full" retirement plan for the American public.

No, it was only meant to be a supplement to other resources for a comfortable retirement and to provide a financial safety net to the older population (those aged 65 or older) during their "final" years.

In fact, upon signing the Act into law on August 14, 1935, Roosevelt said these exact words, "We can never insure 100% of the population against 100% of the hazards and vicissitudes of life, but we have tried to frame a law which will give some measure of protection to the average citizen and to his family against the loss of a job (disability) and against a poverty-ridden retirement". Nothing about this has changed since its inception.

His vision for the retirement program was one of self-financing — contributions made from both the employee and employer. He wanted it to be actuarially sound on its own -- with no money coming out of the U.S. Treasury to pay for benefits. That was a pretty easy "target" to hit, as back then there were some 40 workers to every retiree receiving benefits.

In 1937, Social Security payroll taxes began being automatically taken from paychecks and lump-sum retirement payments began. A gentleman named Earnest Ackerman was the first person to get a lump sum from Social Security. And believe it or not, it was for a grand total of 17 cents! Although it's true that he had only contributed a nickel to the program. My, how times have changed.

Then in 1939, the Social Security program added the provision to add benefits to spouses, minor children and survivors of workers who die early.

And in 1940, retirement benefits were changed from lump sum payments to an ongoing monthly benefit and Ms. Ida Mae Fuller received the first monthly benefit from Social Security. Her monthly check was just $22.40 – completely income tax-free.

It is important to note here that age 65 was the life expectancy in the 1930's. So it wasn't planned that many people would live for decades after turning age 65 like the majority do today.

But interestingly, according to the Social Security website, Ms. Fuller lived to age 100, and over her lifetime, she collected nearly $23,000. For her, I imagine that it was kind of like winning the lottery as she had only contributed $24.75 into the system in the three years prior (1937-1939) to beginning monthly benefits! What a huge financial return that was for her for more than three decades.

Americans should realize a very important fact about the program and changing demographics. When Social Security began, there were some 40 workers paying into the system for every retiree getting benefits. Today it's about four workers contributing for every retiree.

As the Baby Boomers (those born from 1946-1964) retire, because of the enormous size our group, and the relatively few children we have had as a whole, there will only be 2 or 3 workers for each one of us taking monthly benefits. Maybe we all should have had a few more children! In any case, the program looks very different for our generation than how it did when it began.

According to AARP, Mrs. Mary Thompson, a widow, became the one millionth recipient of Social Security benefits in 1944. Six years later in 1950, Social Security added the first cost of living adjustment (COLA) so retirement benefits could better keep pace with inflation.

In 1956, women were granted the right to retire earlier than men (age 62). This was based on the assumption that since most wives were younger than their husbands and that they would like to be retired at the same time.

In 1961, Social Security allowed men to retire early too, starting at age 62, but with a reduced initial benefit from retiring at age 65.

In 1972 annual cost of living adjustments (COLA) were made automatically as well as an across-the-board 20 percent increase in benefits. Social Security also established wage "indexing" of the initial benefit amount upon retirement, in order to ensure that benefits keep up with increases in the standard of living.

During 1977, the government made several changes to Social Security. For example, it raised the payroll tax and reduced benefits slightly to extend solvency of the program.

To combat Social Security's financial problems in 1983, President Ronald Reagan and Tip O'Neill (Speaker of the House) came to a bipartisan agreement that was supposed to put the program on solid ground for decades. It made some big changes in the program.

The 1983 law made those big changes that are still in effect today. It delayed the cost of living increase for six months, increased scheduled rates in payroll taxes, added federal employers to the plan and included members of Congress to the program (what a surprise!). **And for the first time, it started _taxing_ a portion of Social Security income benefits. Yes – taxing some benefits! It also gradually increased the full retirement age from age 65 to age 67.**

Then the government increased the portion of Social Security benefits that were subject to income taxation beginning in 1994 with the passage of the Omnibus Budget Reconciliation Act in 1993.

In the year 2000, the government eliminated the Retirement Earnings Test for those retirees who were at or above the normal retirement age. This allowed seniors who were still working to be able to receive full Social Security benefits instead of having them reduced based on their earnings.

It was also in 2000 that the "file and suspend" strategy was allowed as part of the Senior Citizens Freedom to Work Act. File and suspend will be discussed further in a later chapter.

Kathleen Casey-Kirschling is generally recognized as the first "baby boomer" to receive a Social Security check. That was in 2008. Since some 10,000 Americans are now turning age 65 every single day, the numbers of retiring baby boomers will soon swell to the point where there may be only three workers for every one retiree.

The Social Security program turned 75 years old in 2010 and the average monthly benefit check was about $1,050. Of course, the program has been in the news for years as far as potential changes to the system to ensure it will be there for retirees on an ongoing basis.

So that brings us to the present and the fact that Social Security and Medicare are in the news nearly every week in terms of how the government is going to make changes to ensure the programs can stay in effect for the next 50 years or longer.

Although the political issues are outside the scope of this book, those potential changes could include delaying full retirement ages, eliminating the early retirement ages altogether, have more taxation of Social Security benefits, "means testing" to get any or all of Social Security benefits, limit future cost of living increases, etc.

Nobody can foresee what the future political decisions will be and how that will affect retirees who have already started taking Social Security and those who have not yet filed. But that does not lessen the vital importance of making the best benefit decisions possible based on your own financial circumstances and goals.

How Social Security Benefits Are Funded?

As mentioned before, Social Security was designed as a pay-as-you-go system. In other words, the benefits being paid out to retirees today are being paid for by the contributions of working people and employers who pay into the system through required payroll taxes

(FICA or SECA). The tax is taken right out of an employee's salary or payroll check. You can see exactly how much is taken out on each payroll statement that you get.

These payroll taxes are paid by the employee (6.2% for Social Security (OASDI) plus a 1.45% for Medicare) up to the maximum wage of $118,500 in 2016. This means that an employee earning the Social Security maximum in 2016 would personally contribute $7,342 to Social Security (excluding the 1.45% for Medicare taxes).

Equal amounts of payroll taxes are paid by the employer for a grand total of 15.3% on the first $118,500 for 2016 – of which $14,694 (at the maximum wage) goes into the Social Security fund (the rest of $3,436 is paid to Medicare).

Self-employed people pay the whole 15.3% up to that maximum income level. Just like employees, the total Social Security portion of that (12.4%) could be as much as $14,694 in 2016. Add in the Medicare tax of 2.9% of $3,436 and they are paying in the same $18,130 as the employee and employer pay on a combined basis.

Although the self-employed individual gets to deduct half of that amount on their personal taxes which lessens the tax pain a bit.

Of course, this is on top of federal and state income taxes. Someone earning the Social Security maximum would likely be in the 25% marginal tax bracket (after all tax deductions like mortgage interest, IRA's, etc.)

You might be interested to know that the $118,500 of wages that are subject to the Medicare tax covers about 85% of Americans. In other words, only 15% or so escape contributing more to Social Security beyond that income level. There are proposals to "uncap" the income level or certainly raise the cap to shore up the program's finances for the long term.

Also, beginning in 2013 those individuals earning more than $200,000 (wages) must pay 0.9 percent more in Medicare taxes on earned individual income over $200,000 ($250,000 for married couples filing jointly). There is no earned income cap on this Medicare surtax. There are other new Medicare surcharges (taxes).

Now as much as $14,457 going into the Social Security fund for 2016 may seem like a lot of money – and it is. But let's take a look at what the potential lifetime Social Security retirement benefits might be.

As an example, let's use an employee paying the most possible into the Social Security system during their entire working career. Let's take a hard look at the numbers.

Diane was born in 1946 and was the main bread-winner in her family. For each and every year of her working career, she earned the maximum Social Security earnings which also means that she paid the maximum Social Security taxes each and every year (along with her employers). Her portion of the contributions over the years would have been about $116,000. Her employers would have paid the same amount into the system for a grand total of roughly $232,000.

That is a lot of money contributed to the system. But let's see what her potential benefits might be. Assuming Diane begins receiving her Social Security benefits at her full retirement age of 66, her initial monthly benefit check would be roughly $2,639.

If we also assume that she (or her stay-at-home-spouse) lives to age 100, she/he would collect over $1,730,000 including an annual COLA (cost of living adjustment) assumed here to be 2.8%. We will even ignore the very valuable spousal benefits here and just focus on Diane's benefits for the purpose of making this point.

Now most people don't live to age 100 (and a few do live longer), but if she (or her husband) only lived to their joint life expectancy of 92, she would have collected over $1,180,000 over that time (using the same assumptions). Joint life expectancy means that it is actuarially likely that one or both of them will live at least that long.

That sounds like a pretty good deal. She and her employers put in about $232,000 over her working career and she could take out about five times or even much more than that (depending upon how long she and/or her husband lives). Doesn't that sound a bit like a Bernie Madoff-type Ponzi scheme?

The other side of the coin is that is if both she and her husband died in a car crash before she retired, there would be no retirement benefits from Social Security. They would not have gotten a dime in monthly Social Security retirement benefits – unless there were children who were still minors.

Or let's say that they both passed away before she turned age 73. In this case, they would have not even received the retirement benefit of the $232,000 that she and her employers contributed to the system (breakeven). Although she would have gotten about double what she personally contributed since her employers paid in half of that figure.

Further on in this book, we'll pick up our discussion of maximizing your potential benefits, but for now, I just wanted to make the point that generally, if you live anywhere near your life expectancy, you will receive many more benefits than you personally ever contributed into the system.

That is not to say that there are not some big problems in funding Social Security benefits that lie ahead for retirees. Of course, that's what all of the discussion is about – keeping the system solvent for current retirees and the generations to follow.

Again, when the Social Security program began, there were some 40 workers paying into the system for every retiree collecting benefits. Way back then the life expectancy was only about age 65. Yup, that's the same age people could start receiving their retirement benefits. But the odds weren't great that they would live to get many years of benefits – certainly not the average person.

But today, with decades of amazing medical advances, the life expectancy of a 65 year old male is now almost 85 – and it continues to rise. That's a retirement that is expected to last 20 years longer than when the Social Security program started.

How Are Your Social Security Benefits Calculated?

So let's look at how your own Social Security retirement benefits will be calculated.

For starters, to be eligible for Social Security, you must have paid into the system through a Social Security covered job (FICA withholding) earning at least 40 credits. One can earn a maximum of 4 credits in a year. So in effect, you must have at least 10 years of countable wages in a job where you have contributed to the system.

In 2016, to earn one credit towards your 40 minimum, you need to have had wages of at least $1,260 in a quarter. So a person earning four times that amount in 2016 ($5,040) will have earned 4 credits for the year. You cannot earn more than 4 credits in a year – no matter how much earned income you have.

But as you will see in a moment, higher earnings (and therefore more contributions into the system) will increase the levels of your future retirement income benefits.

Once someone has become eligible for benefits (through getting their 40 credits), they have become "fully insured". Once you are fully insured your future retirement benefits are based on a formula that takes into account their highest 35 years of earned income of which FICA taxes were withheld. If someone hasn't worked for 35 years in a covered job, the missing years will be given a zero (since they made no contributions those years).

For those who worked more than 35 years, the lowest earning years will not be counted. So if someone worked 42 years, the lowest 7 years would be dropped off the calculation – leaving the highest 35 years of income.

There is no question about the earnings formula being complicated. But you will never have to calculate this for yourself. I just want to let you know what is happening behind the scenes when Social Security is calculating your retirement benefits.

Social Security stopped mailing out annual statements to everyone in 2011 (but re-started mailing in 2014 for those age 60+ after public outrage), but you can find an "estimation" of your own Social Security retirement benefits 24/7 by going to the website below and click on the link that says "Get Your Social Security Statement Online". You can register by following the simple directions. Again, the benefits shown are only estimates -- unless you are subject to WEP or GPO which will be discussed later in this book.

Just go to: **www.ssa.gov** and follow the instructions. Once you see your statement, check it for accuracy. Make sure there are no incorrect or missing years of earnings (if there should not be). The Social Security Administration will correct any wrong or missing information if you provide proof with written documentation.

To find out your estimated retirement benefits, click on the link "Estimate Your Retirement Benefits" on the same website. I'll describe how they calculate your benefits below, so that you will understand how it works. And I won't bore you with all of the specifics of "indexing" earnings. But I do get this one question often. Since wages have grown over the years, how does that fact play into the retirement benefit calculation?

For example, forty years ago in 1973, the maximum Social Security wage for contributions was $10,800 (as opposed to $118,500 in 2016). So someone who earned the maximum income or more in 1973, would be credited with about $55,000 toward their Average Indexed Monthly Earnings (AIME). It's an adjustment that is meant to take into account how wages have risen over the decades.

So the 35 highest earning working years are "indexed" (adjusted) and in effect made more current with inflation (except the years after you turn age 60 which are NOT indexed). Those 35 years are added together and then divided by 420 months (35 years x 12 months) to come up with your AIME.

The AIME figure is then used as a basis to calculate your Primary Insurance Amount (PIA). This is a key number! Your primary insurance amount (PIA) is the amount of your monthly Social Security benefit you will get if you begin your benefits at your full retirement age (FRA). (This will be explained later). There's another one of those Social Security acronyms. Sure are lots of acronyms here, aren't there?

But there is another calculation that takes place before coming up with your PIA as Social Security tries to "equalize" benefits or make the system "fairer" for all retirees.

Again, your PIA is the base amount of benefit that the retiree will receive if they begin benefits at their full retirement age (FRA). PIA is the figure that also determines the amount your monthly benefit will be lowered if one takes early retirement... or raised when one delays beginning their Social Security income.

Here's an example of how that final part of the PIA calculation works. Stephen was born in 1954 and enjoyed a very successful business career from the moment he opened his first restaurant. He earned more than the Social Security maximum every year of his career (so he paid the maximum contributions to the system annually). So his AIME was $9,431 (the maximum AIME in 2016).

The formula breaks that AIME figure into three dollar amount parts that are often referred to as "bend points" (which are also indexed to inflation) and each part gets multiplied by a different factor (percentage rate).

The first $856 dollars (for someone turning 62 in 2016) of his (and everybody's) AIME amount gets multiplied by 90% (the lowest level weighs more heavily than the other two levels) which results in $770. As you will see later on, if you have a pension from an employer that did not withhold FICA taxes under the WEP provisions, this first bend point could be reduced to only 40% rather than the 90%.

The next $4,301 of his AIME amount gets multiplied by 32% which results in $1,377. Finally, the highest earning portion of $4,274 of his AIME is multiplied by just 15% for $641. Remember that Stephen has the highest AIME allowed based on his high annual career earnings but the highest portion of his income levels counts the least toward computing his PIA.

So let's take a look at how his $9,431 AIME (2016) determined his primary insurance amount (PIA):

The first $856 dollars of your AIME x 90% = $770
The next $4,301 dollars of your AIME x 32% = $1,377
The final $4,274 dollars of your AIME x 15% = $641
                                Total PIA = $2,788

Why does Social Security calculate your AIME? Why do they weigh your higher income levels less by multiplying those levels with lower percentage rates?

I'm not sure, but I imagine that it is to "equalize" the system so those who had lower incomes during their working years would see more of their past income replaced with Social Security than those with much higher incomes. Let's put some earnings numbers on this.

Again, the Social Security benefit is meant to replace 90% of the first $10,272 average annual wage inflation adjusted earnings plus 32% of your AIME income from $10,272 - $61,884. Then add another 15% of those inflation adjusted earnings from $61,884 to $113,720 (based on 2013). (Above figures were based on someone turning age 62 in 2016 and are adjusted higher for 2017 and beyond.)

Your monthly retirement benefit may be based on your PIA (Primary Insurance Amount) but the amount of the check you will actually receive may be higher or lower than that figure – depending upon when you start taking benefits.

Update: A person who had maximum-taxable earnings in each year since age 22, and who retires at age 62 in 2016, would have an AIME equal to $9,431. Based on this AIME figure and the 2016 bend points of $856 and $5,157, their PIA at full retirement age would equal $2,788. This person would receive a reduced early retirement benefit based on the $2,788 PIA. Their first COLA adjustment this individual could receive is the one effective for December 2017.

I would like to add something to this part of the book that is affecting my own PIA as a tax-savvy business owner in my early years.

Business owners like to take advantage of every single legal tax deduction available to them in order to reduce their current taxation.

Most all of us were taught the prudence of reducing our current taxes to the lowest amount allowed by law. However, even as a professional financial planner, it never really occurred to me how keeping our taxable income low, also would keep our future PIA low since we make FICA contributions based on our taxable income. And a lower PIA means a lower future Social Security income – even if we delay taking it until age 70.

Although I am not suggesting those business owners avoid reducing their taxable income to below $118,500 (FICA maximum income in 2016), you should seriously consider ways to make up for those reductions in your guaranteed Social Security retirement payments.

There are several tax-deductible (for taxable retirement income) or non-deductible (for TAX-FREE retirement income) financial planning options that I use for my clients to help them in this regard that are beyond the scope of this book. However, I do discuss them quite extensively in my "Stress-Free Retirement Planning" book (for those STILL SAVING for their retirement) that is available on Amazon.

Full Retirement Age (FRA) for Social Security

Let's start with what your own (and spouses) FRA would be, which is based on the year that you were born. You may remember from earlier in this book that in 1977, Congress enacted a law to gradually raise the Social Security retirement ages from the original age 65. You can see this law's retirement ages on the chart below.

Of course, you can still retire early (age 62) and begin receiving reduced (not the 100% PIA that you would get if you waited until full retirement age) Social Security benefits for the rest of your life (and your spouses too). We'll look at this in a moment.

Full Retirement Age (FRA) is based on the <u>YEAR</u> of your birth:

The Year You Were Born	Your Full Retirement Age is:
• 1943-54	66
• 1955	66 and 2 months
• 1956	66 and 4 months
• 1957	66 and 6 months
• 1958	66 and 8 months
• 1959	66 and 10 months
• 1960 and later	67

Taking Early Retirement Benefits

A covered worker is considered eligible for Social Security at age 62. More specifically, it is the first FULL month that one has turned age 62. So if you were born on Feb 9th, you would be eligible for benefits in March.

If you begin receiving benefits at age 62 (the earliest you can take Social Security retirement benefits) your initial benefit will be lower… and it will be for the rest of your life. If you delay taking your benefits beyond your full retirement age (FRA), your initial benefits will be increased. More about this in a few moments.

Why would you get a lower monthly benefit check if you take early Social Security? Well, by taking benefits before your FRA, you will be receiving as much as five more years of checks.

The middle column of the chart below shows, how if your FRA is 66 (based on your year of birth), your benefits would be reduced to beginning your Social Security benefits at the various ages of 62 through your full retirement age. The column on the far right shows the same thing (by taking early benefits) if your FRA is 67.

Apply for S.S.at age	If your FRA is 66	If your FRA is 67
62	75.0%	70%
63	80.0%	75%
64	86.7%	80%
65	93.3%	86.7%
66	100%	93.3%
67		100%

So if your full retirement age (FRA) is 66 and you want to begin taking your Social Security benefits at age 64, you will only get 86.7% of your PIA (primary insurance amount). If you wait until age 65 to start getting your monthly checks, you will get 93.3% of your PIA. And if you wait until your full retirement age, you would get 100% of your PIA. The new laws DO NOT change anything on taking early benefits.

The exact formula for reducing your benefits after your 62nd birthday (but before your FRA) is that your primary insurance amount is reduced by 5/9ths of one percent (.00555%) for each of the first 36 months after turning age 62 and 5/12ths of one percent (.004167%) for each of the next 12 months. Actual dollar amounts are always rounded down to the nearest dollar.

Given all that you just read about the substantial reduced benefits that are part of the deal when taking Social Security at age 62, it really surprised me when I learned that some 26% people decided on this option in 2011. And about 78% of retirees began collecting benefits <u>before</u> they hit their full retirement age (FRA).

Think about that for a moment. Over three-fourths of retirees have decided to slash their guaranteed Social Security retirement income by up to 25%-30% for the rest of their lives. That may or may not be a mistake as we'll discuss in a later chapter, but to me, that is a startling statistic. What do you think about this statistic?

Social Security can tell you exactly how much of your PIA you will lose on a monthly basis for the rest of your life, by beginning your benefits at any point between age 62 and your full retirement age.

Let's circle back for a moment and discuss the point mentioned earlier about how when one starts taking Social Security benefits early that they could receive up to five years more checks (depending upon your FRA).

Someone born in 1960, or thereafter, has a FRA of age 67. By taking benefits at age 62, they will get five more years of monthly checks – but those checks will start off being only 70% of one's PIA… and will forever be lower.

The actuaries (mathematicians) will tell you that if you die at your life expectancy you will get the same total amount of actual dollars whether you take a much lower monthly check that begins at age 62, or if you wait and get your full PIA by waiting until your full retirement age.

The Social Security actuaries use "gender neutral" life expectancy, but we all know that in general, women live longer than men. According to their actuaries, any person aged 62 today has a life expectancy of age 82.

Although none of us know when we will take our last breath on earth, if you are in great health at that age, and especially if you are a woman, the odds are very much in your favor that you will live considerably beyond that age – perhaps well into your 90's.

Let's assume that Mike, who is 62, has earned the Social Security maximum for his entire career and begins taking his benefits right away which are reduced to $1,672 monthly to start. Deborah, who also has the highest AIME possible, waits until her FRA of age 66, and will get her full PIA of $2,490 monthly (including assumed COLA's).

Mike will have received nearly $84,000 in benefits before Deborah gets her first check – but her check is much larger so it won't take too many years before her cumulative benefits will equal his. This is what is called the "crossover" or breakeven point.

If COLA's (cost of living adjustments) are <u>not</u> taken into account, this will happen at age 82 or so. But that is not how the Social Security system works in real life.

In the real world, for most years there will be an annual inflation adjustment or additional increase made to both of their monthly checks. The increase is what Social Security says it will be for any particular year, but the increase is the SAME percentage for everyone. So if the increase is 3.1% one year, Deborah will get a much bigger "raise" since her monthly check is bigger to begin with.

If we were to assume a fixed 2.8% annual COLA (which will not be the case since some years there may be no COLA at all and others a very different figure – higher or lower), the crossover point will be reduced to about age 75. Again, that is the age where Mike's and Deborah's <u>cumulative</u> Social Security benefits have reached the same level (about $339,000) since receiving their checks.

Deborah's check will always be larger and will have larger

increases due to any COLA's. The longer they both live, the more cumulative (total) benefits Deborah will enjoy. If they both lived to age 95, she would have received more than $250,000 more total dollars than Mike if we assume an annual COLA of 2.8%. That's a substantial amount of money that, for most people, would have a major impact on their retirement lifestyle and perhaps even more important... their peace of mind.

As you have just seen, your initial monthly benefit amount will also be the basis of your cost of living adjustments (COLA's), so choosing your starting date will have another big ramification – how well you fare against future inflation. And if you (or your spouse) live a long life, it will surely affect your total benefits received – perhaps by a very wide margin.

Below is a listing of historical COLAs received in 1975 through 2013 and are courtesy of the Social Security website. The COLA increase for 2014 was 1.5% and was 1.7% for 2015. It is 0.0% for 2016!

Historical Automatic Cost-Of-Living Adjustments

July 1975 -- 8.0%	January 1995 -- 2.8%
July 1976 -- 6.4%	January 1996 -- 2.6%
July 1977 -- 5.9%	January 1997 -- 2.9%
July 1978 -- 6.5%	January 1998 -- 2.1%
July 1979 -- 9.9%	January 1999 -- 1.3%
July 1980 -- 14.3%	January 2000 -- 2.5%[1]
July 1981 -- 11.2%	January 2001 -- 3.5%
July 1982 -- 7.4%	January 2002 -- 2.6%
January 1984 -- 3.5%	January 2003 -- 1.4%
January 1985 -- 3.5%	January 2004 -- 2.1%
January 1986 -- 3.1%	January 2005 -- 2.7%
January 1987 -- 1.3%	January 2006 -- 4.1%
January 1988 -- 4.2%	January 2007 -- 3.3%

January 1989 -- 4.0%	January 2008 -- 2.3%
January 1990 -- 4.7%	January 2009 -- 5.8%
January 1991 -- 5.4%	January 2010 -- 0.0%
January 1992 -- 3.7%	January 2011 -- 0.0%
January 1993 -- 3.0%	January 2012 -- 3.6%
January 1994 -- 2.6%	January 2013 -- 1.7%

[1] The COLA for December 1999 was originally determined as 2.4 percent based on CPIs published by the Bureau of Labor Statistics. Pursuant to Public Law 106-554, however, this COLA increase was effectively 2.5 percent.

Delaying Starting Your Social Security Benefits

Just as there is a "penalty" for beginning to take your Social Security benefits before your FRA (full retirement age), there is an attractive "carrot" to delay your monthly benefits. At your full retirement age, your PIA (primary insurance amount) is increased by 8% for every year you delay beginning to take your benefits to a maximum of age 70. There are NO changes to this with the new law.

It's called "delayed credits". You can see by the chart below that if your full retirement age is 66, by waiting until you turn 70 to begin taking benefits, your PIA will be 32% larger... for the rest of your life!

Likewise, if your FRA is age 67, your PIA will increase to 124% of what it would have been if you began taking benefits at age 67.

What if your FRA is in between those years like mine is? Well the delayed credits dollar increase works on a pro-rata basis. For example, my year of birth was 1957, so my FRA is age 66½. So if I wait until age 70 to begin taking Social Security my monthly retirement benefit will be 28% larger than if I started at age 66½. But if I don't want to wait that long, and begin taking benefits at age 68, my benefits would be 112% of my PIA. But personally, I am going to wait until age 70.

My brother was born in 1958, so his FRA is age 66 and eight months. If he waits until age 70 to begin taking benefits, his PIA will be increased to 126⅔%. But if he doesn't want to wait that long, and he begins taking benefits at age 68, his benefits would be 110⅔% of his PIA.

So don't worry, the software can easily figure out (down to the month) how much your delayed credits would be, by beginning your monthly Social Security income at any time beyond your FRA. There is no reason whatsoever to delay receiving your benefits beyond age 70, as you would just be missing out on getting each and every month of your maximum benefits.

Apply for your Social Security benefits at age:	Your benefit will be this % of your PIA if **your FRA is 66**:	Your benefit will be this % of your PIA if **your FRA is 67**:
66	100%	93.3%
67	108%	100%
68	116%	108%
69	124%	116%
70	132%	124%

So we have discussed how your primary insurance amount (PIA) is calculated with the AIME formula applied to your career earnings. We also have seen how your full retirement age (based on the year of your birth) works and how taking early or delayed benefits will affect your Social Security benefits for the rest of your life.

Less than 4% of retirees begin taking their benefits between the ages of 67 and 70 and gain the advantage of a much larger check for the rest of their lives. In many cases, the retiree really doesn't have much of a choice due to their financial circumstances.

But I would venture to guess that many retirees in the upper middle class income ranges have made their filing decision "by default", with no real retirement income professional advice or financial planning expertise.

With some creative planning that will be discussed further in the book, they are missing out on $100,000's of extra retirement income over their (and perhaps a spouse's) lifetime – and lower taxes.

By not taking benefits right away, you could increase your guaranteed lifetime Social Security annual income by up to 75%-80%. At the very least, it's worth taking the time to plan with an expert.

As we'll discuss further in this book, you may find that by delaying your benefits, you can also REDUCE your taxable income and therefore the taxes that you will have to pay for decades during your retirement. Again, the decision on when to file and begin getting Social Security checks should not be made without fully considering all of your retirement income, assets, tax-bracket, risk adverseness and more.

Many people take early benefits (before their FRA) and want to... or need to continue working on either a full or part-time basis. And depending upon how much one earns in their employment, they could find a nasty surprise. So if you plan to continue working and collect Social Security prior to your FRA, you need to know how the rules work – it is called the "Earnings Test".

You should also know that there are absolutely NO penalties of any sort for those people who want to continue working beyond their full retirement age (FRA) and begin collecting Social Security benefits at the same time. The only time there might be adverse benefit consequences is when one continues to work while collecting Social Security earlier than your FRA.

How the "Earnings Test" Works

Again, the retirement earnings test applies only to people below their full retirement age (FRA). Social Security will withhold benefits if your earnings exceed a certain level. This level is called the retirement earnings test "exempt amount", and if you start collecting benefits before your FRA. There are NO changes to this under the new rules.

If Wayne starts collecting Social Security benefits before his FRA, but earns less than the annual exempt amount, then he has nothing to worry about as the earnings test does NOT apply in this case.

There are two different exempt amounts that may apply — one is a lower amount in years before the year you attain FRA and the other is a higher amount in the year you actually attain FRA. These exempt amounts generally increase annually with increases in the national average wage index.

Social Security determines the exempt earnings amounts using procedures defined in the Social Security Act (2000). For people who have NOT attained FRA during 2016, the annual exempt earnings amount is $15,720. So for every $2 of earnings (wages, commissions, etc.) in excess of the earned income level of $15,720, Social Security will withhold $1 of your benefits.

If Jack earned $20,720 of earned income while taking Social Security benefits before his FRA, his income would be $5,000 over the earnings test amount. So Social Security will withhold $2,500 ($5,000 multiplied by 50%) from his benefits.

Here's another example showing more specifically how the withholding of benefits occurs. Let's say that Sam files for Social Security benefits at age 62 in January 2016 and his monthly benefit will be $600 ($7,200 for the full tax year).

During 2016, Sam plans to work and will earn $22,400 ($6,680 above the current $15,720 limit).

Social Security would withhold $3,340 of Sam's Social Security benefits ($1 for every $2 he earned over the limit). To do this, Social

Security would withhold ALL benefit payments from January 2016 to June 2016. Beginning in July 2016, he would receive his full $600 benefit and this amount would be paid to him each month for the rest of the year.

When Sam stops working or attains his FRA, Social Security will recalculate his benefits to adjust for the monies they had withheld to make him whole. So one doesn't really lose benefits altogether, but don't count on getting 12 months of Social Security in any year that you earn more than the current limit if you are under your FRA.

For people younger than full retirement age during the whole year

If your monthly Social Security check is:	And you earn	You will receive annual Social Security benefits of:
$700	$15,720 or less	$8,400
$700	$20,000	$6,260
$900	$15,720 or less	$10,800
$900	$20,000	$8,660
$1,100	$15,720 or less	$13,200
$1,100	$20,000	$11,060

Social Security will ask you to estimate your income at the beginning of the year and will base its withholding on that estimate. Any differences are made up the following January, after your W-2 income has been reported. I usually encourage people to overestimate their earnings (if it is variable like real estate commissions, etc.).

Of course, many people will work for a period of months prior to their FRA birthday. For example, if Dianna's birthday is in August and her FRA is age 66, what happens if she works the first part of the year (prior to her turning FRA) and then begins collecting Social Security at FRA (August)?

Unless she has very high income, she would likely not be penalized at all since in the year of your FRA, there is a much higher earnings test level. For people who are attaining their full retirement age during 2016, the annual exempt amount is $41,880. This higher exempt amount applies only to earnings made in months prior to the month of attaining their FRA.

In the year that you attain your FRA, Social Security withholds $1 in benefits for every $3 of earnings in excess of the higher exempt amount. That's $3 in this case and not the lower $2 amount for the earlier years. Earnings in or after the month you reach FRA do not count toward the retirement test at all.

Here's an example of withholding benefits for working during the year that you attain FRA. Please remember that only wages and commissions count (earned income) -- not income from investments, real estate rent, business dividends, etc.

Jane is not yet at full retirement age at the beginning of the year, but she will reach it in November 2016 with her PIA calculated at $2,000 a month. Jane will earn $53,880 in the ten months from January through October. During this working period, Social Security would withhold $4,000 ($1 for every $3 earned above the $41,880 limit). So with $52,080 in earnings prior to attaining FRA ($12,000 over the earnings test limit), Jane would have $4,000 of benefits withheld ($12,000 divided by $3).

To do this, they would withhold her first two checks of the FRA year ($4,000 divided by her $2,000 PIA = 2 months). Beginning in March 2016, Jane will receive her full $2,000 benefit, and this amount will be paid to her each month for the remainder of the year.

Again, it is important to note that any benefits withheld while you continue to work are not "lost". Once you reach FRA, your monthly benefit will be permanently increased to account for all of the months in which benefits were withheld. So Jane would be paid the remaining $4,000 dollars in 2016 along with her full 2016 benefits (paid monthly as normal since she has attained FRA – whether she continues to work or not).

Note: Special payments (vacation or sick pay, past commissions, bonuses, severance pay, etc.) for any work done that was prior to getting your Social Security benefits, does NOT count toward the earnings test.

So there is a difference between benefit reductions as a result of the earnings test (which are not permanently lost) and those reductions of benefits due to taking Social Security retirement before your FRA (which are lost forever and can add up to many $10,000's and guarantee smaller actual annual dollar amount of COLA increases with even mild inflation).

It is important to note that if Jane wanted to earn extra Social Security credits by delaying her monthly income benefits (increasing her lifetime income by 8% a year), then she would not begin taking benefits at her FRA. This will be discussed further later on in this book.

To summarize the proceeding pages, if you want to continue to work beyond your FRA, there is no earnings test and absolutely no "loss" of Social Security benefits by working beyond this point.

However, if you decide to take early benefits (before FRA) and make over $1,310 per month of earned income, you will lose $1 in benefits for every $2 earned over the $15,720 earnings test amount (2016). The exception to this rule is during the year that you actually attain your FRA, and then the earnings test level is higher ($41,880 in 2016) and you only lose $1 for every $3 earned above that amount.

By the way, by continuing to work, you may increase your AIME if your income increases your average career earnings. So your benefits would be adjusted to reflect that higher earnings record.

Spousal Benefits

If you've never married, you just need make sure you understand the importance of the life expectancy discussion contained in this section. But if you are divorced or widowed and especially if you are currently married, you should read this section very carefully. There is a lot of vitally important information here that can really help you in making your Social Security filing decisions... the right ones.

Spousal benefits originated in a time very different than today. In earlier generations if was not uncommon for the wife to have no or very little earnings record on her own, as she mostly stayed at home to raise the family.

Do you remember the TV shows "Father Knows Best", "Leave it to Beaver" or "My Three Sons"? Even in the 1950's and 1960's, it was very common that most women remained in the home while the husband was the sole or primary "breadwinner". But many women in their 50's and early 60's now have lived a very different life from those TV moms and have a substantial personal work history.

By and large, many women of the "baby boomer" generation have a significant earnings record in their own right – sometimes much greater than their husband's earnings record. I see that all of the time – the wife's income and earnings record being much greater than her husbands.

In any case, the Social Security program is completely gender neutral. We have already seen that although women typically live longer than men, gender does not play a role in any part of the program benefit calculations – not AIME, not PIA, not FRA… not anything.

NOTE: If a state recognizes common-law marriage, and if a couple meets the state's requirements for such a marriage, Social Security recognizes it as well. Also a recent Supreme Court ruling on the Defense of Marriage Act (DOMA) has changed the rules for gay people who get married in all states. Now that all legally married gay couples are considered married in all states, one key question remains: when did these marriages become legal? Was it the date of the marriage or the date the specific state began recognizing gay marriage? Clients who are affected by this latest change may need to be patient while the Social Security Admin works through this.

The marriage date is ALWAYS important in either heterosexual or same-sex marriages. A spouse must be married one year to collect spousal benefits. A widow(er) must have been married nine months to receive survivor benefits (except if death is due to an accident).

Before we discuss more about spousal benefits, I want to really emphasize our nation's continuing strides in terms of lengthening life expectancy and how this should play a strong role in making your decisions regarding when to begin Social Security benefits.

As a nation, we already are living 18-19 years longer than we did eighty years ago when Social Security began. With amazing medical advances being made every year, I fully expect that the average life span of most healthy baby boomers will be 5 years longer than the next chart indicates. Please think carefully about this.

The chart below shows that a male aged 60 now has a 50% chance of living almost 21 more years... to almost age 81 (or even older) and a woman of the same age has a 50% chance of living to age 84 or older -- about three years longer than the average male.

For example, among males aged 77 today, about half will likely die before age 86 (within 9.05 years) and the other half are expected to live at least another 9 years (or much longer).

Of course, if you are pretty healthy today and your family has a history of living a long life, this could increase your odds of "beating" the table which takes into account Americans of ALL health histories and various lifestyles (smoking, overweight, dangerous hobbies, reckless drivers, too-little exercise, etc.). And again, fully consider medical advances that don't even exist today. Surely, this will add years to the current life expectancy tables.

Even today, a healthy and active 65-year-old woman has a 62% chance of living to age 90 and a 28% chance of living to age 95. So nearly two-thirds of healthy women who have made it to age 65, will live to see age 90 and over a quarter of them will get pretty darn close to age 100. In fact, according to U.S. Census Bureau, there were 53,364 centenarians in 2010. The large majority of them are female. If we fast-forward to 2050, the number of 100 year-olds is estimated to explode to 600,000. Could you... or your spouse be among them?

Let me repeat that in general, women live about three to four years longer than men, and they have 4 times the chance of reaching the age of 85 as the average male does. Believe it or not, if you are college educated, your odds of living to and beyond life expectancy actually increase. But for everyone, and women in particular, (whether single, divorced or married) Social Security decisions should be made with their own and their spouse's likely longevity firmly in mind.

Life Expectancy Table

Age	Male	Female
60	20.64 years	24.08 years
61	19.85	23.27
62	19.06	22.47
63	18.29	21.68
64	17.54	20.90
65	16.80	20.12
66	16.08	19.36
67	15.37	18.60
68	14.68	17.86
69	13.99	17.12
70	13.32	16.40
71	12.66	15.69
72	12.01	14.99
73	11.39	14.31
74	10.78	13.64
75	10.18	12.98
76	9.61	12.34

77	9.05	11.71		
78	8.50	11.10		
79	7.98	10.50		
80	7.49	9.92		
81	7.09	9.33		
82	6.47	8.78		
83	6.14	8.29		
84	5.74	7.79		
85	5.36	7.32		
86	5.00	6.87		
87	4.66	6.43		
88	4.35	6.02		
89	4.07	5.64		
90	3.81	5.29		
91	3.57	4.96		
92	3.35	4.61		
93	3.15	4.26		
94	2.96	3.93		
95	2.78	3.63		
96	2.62	3.38		
97	2.47	3.18		
98	2.32	3.02		
99	2.19	2.82		
100	2.07	2.61		
101	1.96	2.42		
102	1.86	2.23		
103	1.76	2.06		
104	1.66	1.89		
105	1.57	1.74		
106	1.48	1.60		

107	1.39	1.47	
108	1.30	1.36	
109	1.22	1.25	

It's no secret that medical technology is constantly evolving. With monthly advances in all phases of healthcare, scientists continue to develop more ways to increase our longevity. Medical professionals work to prevent diseases and help patients suffering from diseases and other debilitating impairments, extending their lifespan. Even the healthier patients benefit by living well past what they used to.

Though often taken for granted until a medical scare, Americans value their lives and most of us go to great lengths to ensure that we live as long as possible. There seems to be no limit to what scientists and doctors can come up with and the speed of these innovations continue to increase and amaze. To live longer, we will go as far as having artificial or animal organs and other vital parts made out of aluminum, titanium and even plastics, inserted into our bodies.

We could someday become almost "semi-robotic" – something like the Six-Million Dollar Man (the 1970's hit TV show). Artificial hearts, lungs and other organs and tissues are constantly improving, becoming more dependable and increasingly common. These healing advances help the quality of our lives and new drug and surgical innovations boost our average longevity. Despite the fact that these medical innovations and advancements may cause patients to perhaps become more medically "mechanical", doctors and scientists make it their goal to improve overall health and extend life.

Even now, scientists are developing new lifesaving prescription drugs and even artificial blood as they continue to find nearly infinite possibilities to lengthen life - and at whatever cost. These scientists are continually able to lengthen what we originally thought were the limits of longevity. Are they going too far? That is a question for another day, but there is no question that amazing medical advances will continue to increase our life expectancy. Some say that average longevity may increase by as much as two years every decade or so.

Why did I go into such a longwinded, perhaps overblown discussion about longevity? Because as a professional financial planner, I cannot tell you how many times a prospective client has come into my office wanting a second opinion of the retirement plan that another advisor had put together for them – sometimes years ago.

And do you know what I see 30%-40% of the time? I see a retirement income plan that is based on both of the spouses passing away at age 85 or perhaps before age 90. That, in my humble opinion is a recipe for disaster. I mean, really?? Would you want to rely on a retirement plan that is likely to "expire"… before you do?

I could not sleep at night with a retirement income plan that was not meant to last until at least age 95 (for the youngest and healthiest spouse). All of the retirement plans that I put together are meant to last and perform beyond age 100. Shouldn't yours?

OK, so hopefully you are now thinking in terms of "what if I (or my spouse) lives to my (our) life expectancy… or even well beyond that point"? Although this line of thinking should extend to all areas of passive retirement income, this book focuses on Social Security. So let's get back to spousal benefits in Social Security.

More on Spousal Benefits

The Social Security system provides significant benefits to the "lower-earning" spouse – whether male or female. The lower earning spouse can receive benefits that are based on their own work history and earnings records, or that of their spouse. To be more accurate, the lower earning spouse will receive benefits based on their own record, but a dollar amount would be added to bring their monthly benefit check up to the same level of what their spousal benefit is.

How does one qualify for the spousal benefit?

Under most circumstances (there are exceptions when young or disabled children are involved) you must be at least 62 and have been married to your spouse for at least one year (or you and your spouse are the natural parents of a child together).

You should also know under both the old and new rules that you cannot file for spousal benefits until your spouse has filed for their own benefits. However, that spouse may have used the "file and suspend" that will be discussed later. Nor can you claim spousal benefits when you have already claimed your own benefit (based on your own PIA) if your own PIA is more than 50% of your spouse's PIA.

So what is the spousal benefit? Spousal benefits are always based on the higher earning spouse's PIA. The lower-earning spouse will get 50% of the higher earner's PIA benefit -- if the spouse waits until their own FRA to begin receiving spousal benefits. The spousal benefit will be reduced if the spouse takes benefits before their own FRA.

Even if the higher earning spouse takes early benefits, the spousal benefit is always based on his PIA. His benefits will be reduced for taking early retirement, but not the spouse's (as long as she is at FRA). However, there will not be any delayed credits for the spouse if the higher earning spouse delays collecting benefits beyond that spouse's FRA. Spousal benefits are ALWAYS based on the higher earner's PIA.

For example, if Leonard is the higher earning spouse and his PIA at full retirement age (66) is $2,000, then his wife's spousal benefit will always be based on that figure. If he decides to take early retirement at age 62, his own benefit will be reduced by 25% to $1,500. But his wife's spousal benefit is unaffected and is still based on his PIA of $2,000.

Likewise, if he delays receiving benefits until age 70 and allows his own benefit to continue growing, his wife's spousal benefit will still be based on his PIA of $2,000. The most she can get is half of his PIA if she begins collecting at her own FRA. If she decides to take benefits earlier, her monthly check would be reduced. And there is no financial benefit or incentive for her to wait for spousal benefits beyond her own FRA.

In some circumstances it might make sense for the lower earning spouse to file for spousal benefits at their FRA while letting their own benefits grow with delayed credits (based on their own PIA) and then switch to their own benefit at age 70.

Let's put some more numbers to this concept as an example. Debbie was the high earner and her own PIA is $2,100. Her husband Dick's PIA is $850. They are both at FRA. Debbie wants to file and suspend her own benefit to earn delayed credits (this will be discussed more fully later on).

Since Dick has attained his FRA, he could get his full PIA of $850... or get half of Debbie's PIA ($1,050). In actuality he would get his own PIA of $850 PLUS an additional $200 to bring his monthly benefit to $1,050 (which is half of Debbie's $2,100 PIA). You get the higher amount possible – your own PIA or half of your spouse's PIA at FRA.

Even if Dick had no earnings record of his own, he would still get half of Debbie's benefit since it is higher than zero.

However, if Dick filed for spousal benefits at age 62 instead of his FRA, he would only get 35% of Debbie's PIA or just $735. Taking early benefits may or not be the best idea but it would still be more than taking his own early retirement benefit (75% of his PIA of $850 which would net a lower benefit of $637.50).

Again in actuality, his own benefit would be brought up to equal his spousal benefit from Debbie. And like everything else in figuring Social Security benefits, if Dick applied for spousal benefits anytime between his age 62 and his FRA, the benefit amount would be prorated (down to the month) between 35% and 50% of Debbie's PIA.

Even though Debbie is delaying her own Social Security benefits to age 70 to increase her lifetime monthly check, this will not affect her PIA or the amount of spousal benefits that Dick will get.

You should also remember that Dick's spousal benefit will NOT increase due to Debbie's delayed credits for waiting until age 70 to begin receiving her Social Security benefits. His spousal benefit is based on her PIA alone. Spousal benefits never get 8% delayed credits.

A husband can collect spousal benefits based on his wife's earning record (PIA) and vice-versa but spouses are not permitted to collect spousal benefits off each other's benefit simultaneously.

Under the new laws, if you qualify for both your own retirement benefit as well as the benefit based on your spouse ("IF" they have already filed), and you claim a benefit <u>prior</u> to your age 70, you will have been "deemed" to have filed for the other benefit too. And you cannot make any changes thereafter. So "if" a spouse has already filed, entitling the other spouse to a spousal benefit, that spouse will be deemed to be filing for both benefits (their own and spousal). (You do not have a choice about this).

Social Security doesn't want you to file early (before FRA) with one benefit and have the other benefit grow.

The new laws will change this option for those who are NOT age 62 or older by the end of 2015. However, if you are age 62 by the end of 2015, you can file for a spousal benefit with a "restricted application" and allow your own benefit to grow with the delayed credits until age 70 and then switch to your own higher benefit at that point. We will discuss this in depth later on.

Social Security Benefits for Divorced Spouses

Although lawmakers in 1935 could have had no idea how prevalent divorce would be fifty or sixty years after the Social Security program was enacted, they provided for divorced spouses with benefits that are very similar to what you learned about in the previous section. Again, Social Security has no gender bias so these benefits are available to both men and women alike.

In order to qualify for retirement benefits based on your former spouse's earnings record, you need to satisfy these criteria:

*** You must NOT be currently married to someone else
*** You must be 62 years or older (your "ex" must be 62 or older too)
*** You must have been married to that person for at least 10 years
*** If you are under FRA when you apply, you do not qualify for a
           higher monthly benefit based on your own earnings record

Assuming you meet all of the above conditions, the calculation for divorced benefits works very similar to current spouses. If you have been divorced for at least 2 years, as long as your ex-spouse is age 62 or older, it is not necessary for him/her to have filed for their own benefits in order to receive your divorced spousal benefits. But under the new rules, if you have been divorced for less than 2 years, your ex-spouse must be already receiving Social Security benefits or has filed and suspended by 4/30/2016.

Your former spouse will not even find out that you are collecting benefits under his/her earnings record. Even if you have not spoken to each other in years or know anything about his/her situation, Social Security can still access their records when you provide proof of marriage and give enough information to correctly identify them.

And it doesn't matter how many ex-spouses there may be who qualify for divorced benefits, it will not affect any other person. There is NO effect on any of the ex-spouses, the current spouse or even the worker (usually the ex-husband). Every one of Elizabeth Taylor's many ex-husbands (who qualify per above) could collect Social Security on her high earnings records – even if 3 or 4 of them qualified!

Again, generally speaking, the benefits for divorced spouses work in the same way for as for current spouses. Unless you were born on or before January 1st, 1954, if you, as a former spouse, claim at your FRA, you would get the higher of your own PIA or 50% of your ex-spouse's PIA. If born after that date, you will be deemed as filing for both your own benefit and your divorced benefit and get the higher one. Actually, you'd get your own benefit topped off with the other.

Likewise, if you claim before your FRA, your benefits will be reduced as discussed before (the same with filing for any benefits early). And just like with spousal benefits, you do not get any more benefits (no 8% delayed credits) by waiting beyond your FRA.

If you meet the new age requirements, one very smart strategy to consider in many circumstances is to take the divorced spousal benefit at FRA and delay receiving your own benefit (based on your personal earnings record) to get delayed credits to build your own PIA and a larger monthly income at age 70. This is filing a "restricted application" which will be discussed later and like spousal benefits, subject to the new age rules. This strategy will NOT work if you file for divorced benefits before you reach your FRA.

So many divorced spouses short themselves of many $1,000's of dollars (for the rest of their lives) because they were not aware of spousal benefits for divorced people. You should also know that you cannot claim divorced benefits if you have already claimed your own benefits (based on your own earnings record) and your own PIA is higher than 50% of your ex-spouse's PIA.

Many of the same strategies that we will discuss later on for married couples will work for divorced "couples" who qualify. So if you were married for at least ten years to someone who probably has a higher earnings record than you do, you want to think about Social Security in terms of how you can best use both earnings records to optimize your lifetime benefits.

And without venturing into "relationship counseling", as a financial planner, if you were my client and contemplating getting a divorce within a year or two before the marriage would have turned 10 years old, I would have you carefully consider the ramifications of the potential loss of divorced spousal benefits by getting the divorce "finalized" before you meet the 10 year minimum for these benefits.

It may make good financial sense to delay the divorce decree until just after your 10th anniversary. That caution is especially true for the spouse with a much lower Social Security earnings history and the corresponding lower personal PIA. I'm just saying!

You should also know that divorced benefits STOP if you remarry. So after divorcing your first spouse and you get married to another person you will not qualify for divorced benefits based on your ex-spouses PIA. But you will qualify for current spousal benefits after one year of the new marriage. And one more point. If you get divorced again, you may be eligible for spousal benefits from either of your "ex's" (as long as all of the normal requirements are met)... or you may begin your benefits from your first spouse again.

I will also mention here that if your former spouse has passed on, the divorced survivor benefits work in much the same way (assuming the same requirements as above and you are not remarried before age 60) as what will be discussed next – survivor's benefits.

Survivor's Benefits

Survivor's benefits, also referred to as widow or widower's benefits are based and calculated by using the deceased person's earnings record.

Just like in the cases of spousal and divorced benefits, there are some simple eligibility requirements which are as follows:

***   Your spouse must have been fully insured (had their 40 credits)
***   You must be at least 60 (unless disabled and are age 50 or older)
***   The marriage must have lasted at least 9 months (unless death was caused by an accident)
***   You must not have remarried unless you did so at age 60 or older

More than a few people are under the wrong assumption that if Social Security benefits have not already started... there is NO survivor's benefit. That is patently and absolutely false! If the surviving spouse has not yet begun taking any Social Security benefits and meets the above qualifications, he/she can file for survivor benefits.

I did a Social Security planning webinar for my investment clients a few months ago. The next day I received an email from one of them saying that he was going to elect to receive early benefits in order to protect his wife from losing out on survivor benefits.

Not only was he extremely relieved that he was making a false assumption, but together we worked on a plan to delay claiming benefits until at least full retirement while still "quitting" his job at age 62 (retiring from the office politics). By doing this, his wife will be better protected and they will both enjoy larger checks for the rest of their lives.

How much will the survivor get? This can get a little complicated. It depends on if that spouse took early benefits, waited until their FRA or delayed filing as well as the age when the survivor spouse will begin taking the survivor benefits. Depending on those facts, you could get 100% of what the deceased was already receiving or 82.5% of his PIA (if you are at FRA). You'll get less if you file before your FRA.

Why is there a difference between up to 100% of the current check or 82.5% of his PIA? If the deceased took early Social Security, 82.5% of his PIA could be a bigger amount than his current check. But if he retired at or near FRA or delayed benefits, then the original amount he was receiving would likely be greater than 82.5% of his PIA. Social Security will give you the larger amount as long as you are at FRA. Again, if you start collecting any Social Security benefit before FRA there is always a reduction in what you will receive.

However, if he had NOT already started receiving benefits and was under his FRA, you would receive 100% of his PIA amount. If he was at FRA or older you would get 100% of his PIA as well as any delayed credits earned (if any) up until the date of his passing – assuming you are at FRA.

If you are not already at your FRA, there is a deduction for starting survivor benefits before your FRA as shown on the chart below. Keep in mind that Social Security will always give you the highest benefit that you are entitled to.

But that doesn't mean that there are not some smart planning opportunities to consider delaying survivor's benefits for more lifetime income if you expect to live a long life.

For example, if you have other income or assets to use and are between the ages of 60 and FRA, it might be smarter over the long-term to delay taking benefits. Although you may miss out on a few years of benefits, by delaying your benefits could be substantially higher and you might get many more cumulative benefits if you live well beyond your mid-seventies. Each filing situation is unique.

Let's look at an example. If the original survivor's benefit (PIA) is $2,000 (or $24,000 a year) and you are age 60 at that point, let's look at the two extremes – taking benefits right away (and only receive 71.5% of the original PIA)... or waiting until your FRA at age 66 where you would get 100% of the original benefit. And let's make it a bit more real world by assuming annual COLA's at 2.8% and look at the long-term annual income implications.

Now if you need the income right away because you don't have enough assets or other income with which to live comfortably on, then the next paragraphs are a moot point. But let's take a look.

If you started benefits right away (71.5%) you would get six more years of income but at age 70 your annual benefit would be $22,618. However, if you waited until your FRA, your annual benefit would be almost 50% larger at $31,633 a year including COLA's.

Looking forward to age 80 (assuming the same 2.8% COLAs) by taking early benefits your income that year would be $29,811. But your income could have been $41,694 if you had delayed benefits. At age 95 the annual amounts are $45,110 and $63,091 respectively.

At what age is the breakeven point under this scenario – where you would get more cumulative benefits by waiting to receive survivor's benefits? It's about age 77 in this case. If you can afford it and are likely to live beyond that age – give this some serious thought.

Percent of Survivor's Benefits Received
if Started Before the Survivor's FRA
(percentage of the full 82.5% at FRA)

Age When You Begin Collecting Survivor's Social Security Benefits:	FRA 66	FRA 67
Age 60	71.5%	71.5%
Age 61	76.2%	75.6%
Age 62	81%	79.6%
Age 63	85.7%	83.7%
Age 64	90.5%	87.8%
Age 65	95.2%	91.9%
Age 66	100%	95.9%
Age 67		100%

These rules change if the spouse is still caring for the deceased's child who is under age 16. In this case, the benefit would be 75% of the PIA – but for only as long as the child(ren) are under age 16. When the youngest being cared for hits age 17, then the survivor's benefit ceases until the spouse turns 60 (unless disabled).

If you are already getting Social Security benefits based on your own work record (or a spousal benefit) and are eligible for survivor's benefits, you would notify Social Security and you would get the survivor's benefit if that amount was higher than what your own monthly check is. Of course, your previous check would cease and you would only get the one.

Here are a couple of examples that may make this a little clearer.

Lloyd started taking early benefits when he was 63 (his FRA is 66 when his PIA is $1,600). Because Lloyd started taking benefits before his FRA, he was only getting 80% of his PIA or $1,280. He later died at age 65.

If his wife Gloria was at FRA when he died, she would collect the larger of what he was collecting ($1,280) or 82.5% of his PIA ($1,320).

However, if Lloyd had waited until reaching age 68 to begin benefits, the delayed credits would have added 16% to his PIA and would total $1,856. In this case, Gloria's survivor benefit would be the full amount of what Lloyd was receiving. By the way, if Lloyd was still delaying his own benefits in order to build more delayed credits until age 70, Gloria's survivor's benefit would be calculated based on the delayed credits earned up until the date of Lloyd's death.

Here's another example looking at a couple's situation from many vantage points.

Heather and Clark are both 62 years old and are considering their Social Security options. Clark's retirement benefit (PIA) at full retirement age (66) is $2,400. Clark was another person who was unsure about whether he should file for his Social Security benefit now because he had thought that if he is not collecting Social Security when he died that Heather would not receive any survivor's benefit.

Again this misinformation or rumor is totally false. There is NO requirement that he needs to be already collecting Social Security in order for Heather to receive survivor's benefit (assuming all other requirements are met as stated above).

Let's take a quick look at what Heather's survivor benefit might be under different life circumstances that could happen.

Possibility #1: Clark dies BEFORE ever filing for his Social Security benefits. In this situation, Heather's survivor benefit will be Clark's full PIA, or $2,400 depending upon her age at that point. If Heather files for it at her FRA she would get 100% of his $2,400 PIA. If she filed for the survivor's benefit before then, there is the usual reduction.

If Clark dies before filing, which is something that they were concerned about, Heather will receive $420 a month more by Clark waiting until his FRA ($2,400 vs. $1,980) than if he took early benefits.

Think about it. If Heather lives 30 more years, she would have lost out on over $150,000 ($420 x 360 months) in survivor benefits if Clark filed at 62. And the amount of lost benefits grows even larger if we include COLA's. According to the rules, if Heather files for her survivor benefit at 62 with Clark never filing before he died, she will only get 81% of his PIA or $1,944.

Possibility #2: Clark files for his Social Security benefits as soon as he turned 62... and then immediately dies the next day. Under this circumstance Heather's survivor benefit would be 82.5% of Clark's PIA, which is $1,980 (assuming she waits to her FRA). If she decides to file for it right away (at her age 62), she will receive a reduced benefit of just 81% of the $1,980 which equals $1,603.

Possibility #3: Clark doesn't pass away until just before he would have filed for his benefits at age 70 to accrue delayed credits for both he and Heather's benefit. In this situation, her survivor benefit will gain from all his 8% delayed credits plus all the COLA's. Since Clark never filed for benefits, Heather's survivor benefit will be increased by 32% making it $3,168 ($2,400 x 132%) along with all COLAs. With Heather being age 70 (at her FRA or older) she will get the full $3,168.

In all of the three cases, Heather's survivor's benefit was <u>not</u> affected by Clark's filing or not filing. But there is a huge range of survivor benefits from $1,980 to $3,168 depending on whether Clark files early at age 62 or waits until age 70. Depending upon how long Heather lives, the difference could be hundreds of thousands of dollars over her lifetime.

Let's think about potential strategies here to maximize potential lifetime benefits from Social Security after a death. If the surviving person is between the ages of 60 and their full retirement age and has a long life expectancy, it may be a mistake to claim a survivor's benefit right away. That may be especially true if you are a healthy woman.

If the survivor has other income, it may be best to wait until FRA to begin benefits to get the most allowed. Other times it makes more sense to claim benefits based on your own earnings record at age 62 and then switch to the full survivor's benefit at FRA.

And then there is always the opposite strategy of filing for a lower survivor's benefit right now and then make the one-time change to your own PIA at your FRA (or wait even longer and build your own delayed credits).

Most people and financial advisors alike do not know the next fact. Unlike spousal and divorced benefits, the survivor benefit rules did NOT change with the new law passed in November 2015, so there are some savvy strategies that we can still use.

As I have written before and no doubt will repeat it more than once in these pages, it all comes down to your personal situation and what the numbers reveal given the facts of your circumstances, your likely longevity, other assets and income.

I should also make it clear that when one person of a married couple passes away, there will only be ONE Social Security benefit. That single benefit may be raised to the highest allowed by the current rules, but a survivor cannot collect a survivor's benefit in addition to their own benefit. So if a deceased was collecting $2,300 a month and the survivor was collecting $1,650 a month, the survivor would

REPLACE their own monthly benefit with the larger one. But there will only be one check going forward.

So who says retirees don't need life insurance except for final expenses? Many do need life insurance but don't have nearly enough.

Could the surviving spouse live the same lifestyle with only one monthly check coming in (losing the 2nd check of $1,650 every month)? That's a huge hole in the household budget of nearly $20,000 a year (not including the annual COLAs). And this loss of one of two checks each month could go on for decades if the surviving spouse lives a long time. It could be a financial loss of $100,000's of income over the remaining spouse's lifetime… as well as added financial security and peace of mind.

Unfortunately, many couples do not discuss this very common eventuality beforehand. How many widows (or widowers) do you know who have lived many years after their spouse has passed away?

Before proceeding, I'll make a few more comments on survivor's benefits that you might find interesting.

If a widowed spouse remarries before they turn age 60 (or age 50 if disabled), that spouse is NOT entitled to survivor's benefits based on the deceased spouse's earnings record. I know that love can be blind, but one might be wise to consider putting off the next marriage until they turn 60 if one is just a year or two away from attaining that age.

But if that new marriage ends in divorce, you may be eligible to regain the deceased spouse's survivor's benefits that you were previously entitled to. If the new marriage happens after age 60, there would be no change in the current survivor's benefits. They would continue just as before.

And depending upon your date of birth, there may be some planning strategies that might work to improve the situation, but only if the new spouse's earnings record is substantially higher than that of the former spouse. If this is the case, you might switch over to a spousal benefit based on your new spouse's PIA if that benefit would be more than what you are currently getting.

And if by chance the second spouse passes away before you do, you have the choice (assuming you meet the requirements) of choosing the higher survivor's benefit between the two deceased spouses. Few folks really know how to optimize their benefits!

And there still is the potential to switch to your own benefits (based on your personal PIA with delayed credits until age 70) if that figure would be higher than your existing survivor's or potential current spousal benefit. Each situation is as different as fingerprints, but it always makes perfect sense to check out all of your options.

Taxation of Social Security Benefits

Many people do not realize that they may have to pay income tax on all or part of their Social Security Benefits. Some people are even shocked to find this out.

It wasn't always the case, but the taxation of Social Security benefits started in 1983. The taxation of these retirement benefits changed again in 1994 (and will likely change at least once again).

As you can see from the chart below that those with low provisional income (your adjusted gross income plus 50% of your Social Security benefit(s) plus all tax-exempt interest from municipal bonds) will not pay any taxes on their Social Security benefits. Others will pay income taxes on half of the benefits while the better-off will pay income taxes on 85% of the monthly Social Security benefit.

I would also like to add that the income levels on the chart below have not been adjusted for inflation since 1994 – that's 20 years ago. Certainly $44,000 (and all of the figures below) was worth much more back then that it is today.

So more and more people are being taxed on their Social Security benefits each year as it becomes increasingly easier to attain those income levels. It is very easy to speculate that unless Congress does something it hasn't done in 20 years and change the thresholds, at one point almost everyone will be taxed on their Social Security income.

NOTE: About 37 states do NOT currently tax Social Security benefits. That means 13 states (and some local governments) do tax all or part of our monthly income benefits. Of course, that could always change.

Taxation of Social Security benefits

Your Tax Filing Status	Provisional Income**	Amount of Social Security benefits that are subject to any taxation (I.R.S.)
Married filing jointly	Under $32,000 $32,000 - $44,000 Over $44,000	0% Up to 50% Up to 85%
Single, head of household, qualifying widow(er), married filing separately and living apart from spouse	Under $25,000 $25,000 - $34,000 Over $34,000	0% Up to 50% Up to 85%
Married - filing separately and living with spouse	Over $0	85%

Provisional Income = AGI PLUS one-half of your SS benefit(s) PLUS all tax-exempt interest (muni bonds)

Many people wrongly believe that all of their Social Security check will be taxed at an 85% tax rate – but that's not what the figures on the right side of the above graph mean.

What it is saying is that up to 85% (or 50% if your provisional income is between those figures on the chart) will be *subject to* income taxes – at your marginal tax rate. The other 15% (or 50%) will not be taxed at all by the I.R.S. So for now at least, part of everyone's benefit (or 100% if your provisional income is under $25,000 (single) or $32,000 (filing jointly etc.) is completely income tax-free.

There is some proration of taxes for those with provisional income so let's see how that works with a couple of examples.

Scenario #1: John and Becky have combined Social Security income of $20,000 and their other adjusted gross income is $44,000. They have no tax-exempt interest. Half of their Social Security benefits equals $10,000 so their provisional income is $54,000 ($44,000 plus $10,000). From that we subtract the "allowed" $44,000 and come up with $10,000 as the excess over the base amount. Of that $10,000 of Social Security benefits, 85% is subject to taxation (or $8,500) at their marginal tax rate.

But since they had provisional income between $32,000 and $44,000 we have to include 50% of that $12,000 amount (see chart) and add $6,000 to the $8,500 above to equal $14,500. So they would have to include $14,500 of their $20,000 Social Security benefits in their taxable income. That works out to 72% of their Social Security benefits that are subject to tax.

As you can see from the 2016 tax table below, a couple filing jointly with taxable income under $75,300, puts that couple in the 15% marginal tax rate. You will notice that the first $18,550 of taxable income is only taxed at 10%. All taxable income over that amount (up to $75,300) is taxed at the 15% rate.

So let's take a look at how there is a type of tax surcharge – where you pay higher than the 15%. This might just make you mad, but it's the law. And most people have no idea of how it works.

Scenario #2: Let's pretend that John and Becky had other adjusted gross income of $46,000 ($2,000 more than the $44,000 threshold). So let's run through the numbers once more with their Social Security benefits still at the same $20,000.

Again, they have no tax-exempt interest but half of their Social Security benefit is $10,000 (same as before) so their provisional income is $56,000. From that, we subtract the "allowed" $44,000 and come up with $12,000 as the excess over the base amount. Of that $12,000 in Social Security, 85% is subject to taxation or $10,200.

But they had income between $32,000 and $44,000 so we have to include 50% of that amount and then add $6,000 to the $10,200 to equal $16,200. They would have to include a total of $16,200 of their full $20,000 of Social Security income in their taxable income. Now, 81% of their Social Security is subject to taxes. But keep reading.

One would think that the extra $2,000 of adjusted gross income would add just $300 to their tax bill ($2,000 X 15% tax rate = $300).

But let's see what really happens. For someone getting Social Security who is subject to tax on 85% over the base threshold, a strange "tax bomb" occurs. In scenario #1, the 85% subject to tax was $8,500. In scenario #2 it was $10,200 or $1,700 more.

By adding the $2,000 of additional gross income ($46,000) and the new amount that is subject to taxation ($1,700) we get an additional taxable amount of $3,700 – not $2,000. Applying the 15% tax rate on the full $3,700 means that the couple will pay $555. That is a tax rate of 27.77% on the extra $2,000 of gross income ($46,000 vs. $44,000).

But again, logic would say that if there was $2,000 more income, the increased tax bill would be $300 ($2,000 x 15%). However, the actual increased bill was $555. That is nearly twice the tax rate on these dollars as somebody not collecting Social Security benefits.

Although income taxes are well beyond the scope of this book, for couples with Modified Adjusted Gross Income (MAGI) above $54,000 or when Social Security income is $20,000... this tax bomb "disappears". For single filers, it's about $42,000 with similar benefits.

With as little as $20,000 of MAGI (excluding Social Security) for single filers and $24,500 for joint filers each dollar of extra income might get taxed as if it were $1.50 or $1.85 of income.

In general, the higher your Social Security benefits are compared to your MAGI, the lower your MAGI needs to be to potentially put you in this tax-bomb. By the way, when my mom passed away in 2013, my dad filed as a single in 2014... and his taxable Social Security went UP!

As we will see in a later chapter regarding Social Security advanced tax planning strategies, a $1,000 of IRA income can be very, very different than $1,000 of Social Security benefits as they are treated differently in the current tax system.

Using these advanced strategies might be able to cut your taxable income by more than 50% over your lifetime. That my friend is a BIG deal and another indication of why most people should not make Social Security decisions without expert advice.

Who wants to pay more taxes than the law requires? I like to help my clients use financial strategies and specially designed financial products to exchange IRA dollars for Social Security dollars to reduce taxes. Put another way, it can be possible to increase one's NET spendable income (by reducing taxes) over your retirement years.

So minimizing taxation of your Social Security benefits is another worthy goal. You cannot control the size of your Social Security checks (after age 70) or other pensions. But you can control, to a large extent, how much, the timing of, and from what investment sources you take income to meet your retirement lifestyle goals.

I'll discuss this topic much more later on in the book when I give examples with the Earlys, the Waites and the Bests. I think you will be amazed at how much we can lower taxable income (and thereby increase what you have leftover in your pocket) by making some savvy financial moves. I'll just say for now, that the earlier one makes these financial moves, the more likely we can dramatically improve your retirement years.

2016 Tax Table

2016 Federal Tax Rates and IRS Marginal Tax Brackets

Tax Rate	Single	Married Filing Jointly	Married Filing Separate Returns	Heads of Households
Personal Exemption	$4,050	$4,050	$4,050	$4,050
Std Deduction	$6,300	$12,600	$6,300	$9,300
10%	$0–$9,275	$0 - $18,550	$0–$9,275	$0-$13,250
15%	$9,275–$37,650	$18,551-$75,300	$9,275–$37,650	$13,251-$50,400
25%	$37,651-$91,150	$75,301-$151,900	$37,651-$75,950	$50,401-$130,150
28%	$91,151–$190,150	$151,901-$231,450	$75,951–$115,275	$130,151-$210,800
33%	$190,1501-$413,350	$231,451-$413,350	$115,276-$206,675	$210,801-$413,350
35%	$413,351-$415,050	$413,351-$466,950	$206,676-$233,475	$413,351-$441,000
39.6%	over $415,050	over $466,950	over $233,475	over $441,000

If you plan to continue working while starting Social Security benefits prior to you FRA, keep in mind that your Social Security benefits might push you up into the next tax bracket (and perhaps the tax-bomb just described) – along with getting a reduction of benefits of $1 for every $2 in earnings from work over $15,720.

The point is that income taxes are another reason to consider delaying the start of your Social Security benefits if you want to continue working before you attain FRA.

A common question I'm often asked by folks from around the country is "how do I reduce my income in retirement to minimize my tax bill – especially if I am spending less than my taxable income"?

For some folks, the best answer is to begin converting IRA's and old 401(k)'s, 403(b)'s, etc. to a ROTH IRA over time, where there are no Required Minimum Distributions (RMD's) and proper withdrawals avoid all taxation. And income from a ROTH do not enter the tax calculation of taxation of Social Security benefits. When possible, I like to start (and hopefully finish this conversion) before we begin taking Social Security benefits.

Another potential solution is using annuities for non-qualified (non IRA-type money) money which give you tax deferral (although any withdrawals are taxed as earnings first (until you get to your basis) at ordinary income tax rates. But with annuities – you control how much you withdraw and pay taxes on... and when to do so.

And believe it or not, certain cash value life insurance policies are often the best solution to meet a number of important financial goals while deferring income taxes. And if those funds are never used, the death benefit passes all gains (and more) on a tax-free basis.

Depending upon one's circumstances, I often structure the life insurance policy to give tax-free income. When we can do this, not only is the income tax-free, but it does not affect the taxation of Social Security at all. Proper distributions from a life insurance contract do not even enter into the Social Security taxation calculation, whether you are taking $10,000, $50,000 or $250,000 a year out of your policy. Nor do these proper distributions appear on any tax-form.

Again, just like a ROTH IRA, proper distributions from the life policy (if structured for this) do not even show up on your tax return at all, therefore not pushing you into a higher tax bracket. Nor does either cause your monthly Social Security checks to be taxed, since these distributions do NOT count towards provisional income.

Not even low yielding tax-free municipal bonds can do that, as interest from these bonds avoid federal taxation (and sometimes state taxes too), but they do play a role in determining the taxation of your Social Security benefits.

My books, "**Recession-Proof Retirement**" for those already retired (or close) and "**Stress-Free Retirement Planning**" (for those not needing at least a certain amount of funds for a while... or you will be saving for another 10 or more years from now) really delve into the use of life insurance and its many "living" benefits much more.

I would also mention that reverse mortgages also offer tax-free income that do not get included in the Social Security taxation calculation. However, in general I do not recommend using reverse mortgages at all – unless there is no other financial choice to pay the bills. As a general rule, I like for retirees to hold on to the "option" of using reverse mortgages until their late 70's or 80's, as this gives the property more time to appreciate and the shorter life expectancy increases the monthly payout. To me, it could be a pretty good "plan B" for those who live much longer than they thought they would.

But like all rules of thumb in this book (or any other), there are exceptions as to when to use a reverse mortgage. It all comes down to your own personal circumstances and financial goals.

Two Potential Social Security Gotchas (WEP & GPO)!

There are a couple of potential Social Security provisions that just may affect you or your spouse, so let's mention them here. The **Windfall Elimination Provision (WEP)** came into existence in 1983.

The WEP provision only affects those retirees who have earned a pension from a job where NO Social Security taxes (FICA) were withheld and also worked in a job(s) "with substantial earnings" where Social Security taxes were paid. For example, many local and state government agency employees do not have Social Security withheld from their paychecks. That could mean millions of baby boomers could be affected... and not even know it. NOTE: Military pensions are exempt from WEP reductions. Thank you for your service!

For example, Samuel was a high school teacher for 22 years with a school system that had their own pension plan (and no Social Security taxes were withheld) before he retired from teaching at age 44. Then Sam worked for a major retail chain that withheld Social Security taxes for the next 23 years. If Sam had 30 or more years in jobs (with "substantial earnings") that had FICA taxes withheld, WEP would not affect him. But he only has 23 years, so he will see a WEP reduction in his Social Security retirement benefits. See chart below.

The longer you have worked in a job(s) that was covered by Social Security, the less effect WEP has on your PIA. WEP affects your first AIME "bend point" discussed earlier in this book.

Despite what your annual Social Security statement may say your PIA is, if the above applies to you, you will likely be hit with the WEP reduction when you retire. However, you will have no way of knowing if and how much this provision will reduce your monthly Social Security check by... UNTIL you actually file for benefits. Talk about a surprise when you least expect it!

Why wouldn't this potential reduction show up on your annual benefit projection statement? Because the Social Security Administration has no idea that you have a pension from a job where you did not have FICA taxes withheld.

With today's technology, that should be easy for them to know, but there is no way they can easily go back 35 years and find that out for millions of upcoming retirees. And I doubt it is a priority for them to spend the money and resources on.

In 2015, the biggest reduction to your PIA allowed by the WEP was about $413 per month. And as you know, your PIA determines any early or delayed credits. If you were expecting $2,065 a month (PIA) based on your annual Social Security statement, the maximum WEP penalty could cost you about 20% of your anticipated benefit.

According to the Social Security Administration, substantial earnings is defined as an amount equal to or above the income amounts shown in the table below (where FICA taxes were withheld) for the years from 1937-2015:

Year	Substantial Earnings Amount
1937-1954	$900
1955-1958	$1,050
1959-1965	$1,200
1966-1967	$1,650
1968-1971	$1,950
1972	$2,250
1973	$2,700
1974	$3,300
1975	$3,525
1976	$3,825
1977	$4,125
1978	$4,425
1979	$4,725
1980	$5,100
1981	$5,550
1982	$6,075
1983	$6,675
1984	$7,050
1985	$7,425
1986	$7,825

1987	$8,175
1988	$8,400
1989	$8,925
1990	$9,525
1991	$9,900
1992	$10,350
1993	$10,725
1994	$11,250
1995	$11,325
1996	$11,625
1997	$12,150
1998	$12,675
1999	$13,425
2000	$14,175
2001	$14,925
2002	$15,750
2003	$16,125
2004	$16,275
2005	$16,725
2006	$17,475
2007	$18,150
2008	$18,975
2009	$19,800
2010	$19,800
2011	$19,800
2011	$19,800
2012	$20,475
2013	$21,075
2014	$21,750
2015	$22,050

So, if your earnings from your Social Security-covered job(s) were "substantial" based the table above, it is possible to change the WEP reduction factor, on an increasing scale from the standard 45% reduction (20 years or fewer in Social Security covered jobs) – up through possibly eliminating WEP entirely (with 30 or more years in covered jobs), depending on how many years you've earned those substantial earnings.

As long as you've had those substantial earnings for more than 20 years in a job(s) that withheld FICA taxes, use the table below to determine what your first AIME bend point factor would be. You may remember the normal first "bend point" is 90% of your first $826 (2015). You can refer to AIME calculations from earlier in the book to refresh your memory).

Years Worked with Substantial Earnings in S.S. Covered Jobs	First Bend Point of AIME Percentage Factor
30 or more years	90% of first $826 (WEP has no affect at all)
29	85%
28	80%
27	75%
26	70%
25	65%
24	60%
23	55%
22	50%
21	45%
20 years or less	40%

So if you had twenty or fewer years in a Social Security-covered job (paid FICA taxes) with substantial earnings, your WEP-reduced factor on the first AIME bend point is 40%. For each year more than 20 of substantial earnings, your WEP-reduced factor increases by 5%. If you have 30 or more years of substantial earnings, WEP does not impact your first bend point factor at all – therefore there is no WEP "penalty" and no reduction to your PIA and monthly benefit.

Going back to our high school teacher Samuel, his Social Security check would be reduced by about $289. How did we get to that number? Well, with 23 years of FICA contributions on "substantial" earnings, his first bend point of $826 gets only 55% instead of 90%. Therefore 55% of $826 is $454 instead of the $743 that 90% would be. Subtract $454 from the $743 and you get a $289 reduction in benefits.

Again, the biggest reduction to your PIA allowed by the WEP is about $413 per month even if you have less than 20 years in job(s) covered by Social Security. And the absolute maximum WEP reduction is 50% of your monthly Social Security pension amount (but no more than the $413). The maximum WEP amount for 2016 has not been published as of this edition but it should be within $10 of the $413.

WEP is complicated and a full discussion is beyond the scope of this book. More information is available on the Social Security website, along with calculators to approximate your potential WEP reduction.

What if your pension was paid to you in a lump sum? Social Security will calculate it as if it were being paid to you monthly, so taking a lump-sum pension will <u>not</u> help you escape WEP (or GPO).

How does WEP affect spousal benefits? Phil worked in a job that did not pay into Social Security. He also worked in two Social Security-covered jobs, but did not have 20 years of substantial earnings in those jobs, which means his PIA is reduced by about $413 (2015) for the WEP. Phil's pre-WEP PIA is $1,605. His WEP-adjusted PIA is $1,182. His wife Betsy's spousal benefit, if she waits to file for it at her FRA, will be 50% of $1,182 -- or $591.

Let's look at another situation where Doug worked in a non-Social Security covered job. In this case, Judy's spousal benefit will be based on his WEP-adjusted PIA. Again, Social Security is gender-neutral.

Doug worked in a job that did not pay into Social Security. He also worked in a Social Security-covered job, but did not have 20 years of substantial earnings in that job, which means his own PIA is reduced by about $413 for the WEP. Doug's pre-WEP PIA is $1,701. His WEP-adjusted PIA is $1,278. Judy's spousal benefit, if she files for it at her FRA, will be 50% of $1,278 which equals roughly $639.

You should know that survivor benefits are NOT affected by WEP. But don't think widows and widower's are "in the clear". This is where the Government Pension Offset (GPO) may apply.

The **Government Pension Offset** works in a similar manner to WEP, but it also affects spouses and survivors who otherwise qualify for Social Security benefits... but have their OWN government pensions (lump sum or monthly) and have not contributed into the Social Security program via paying their own FICA taxes. We'll talk about how GPO affects survivor benefits first (Martha) and then give an example of how GPO affects spousal benefits (Lee Ann). In these situations, the spouses will have their spousal benefits reduced by up to two-thirds.

Martha was a successful corporate attorney who retired at her FRA with a PIA of $2,300. Her husband Donald was a police officer for his whole career and never worked in the private sector nor contributed to Social Security. His monthly pension from the police department is $1,900.

Martha lost her battle with ovarian cancer at age 73. If Donald had contributed to Social Security, he would be entitled to a survivor's benefit equal to her PIA (ignoring COLA's for the moment). However, since he paid no FICA taxes, his survivor's benefit is reduced by two-thirds of his own pension amount.

To put numbers to this example, two-thirds of $1,900 is about $1,250. Social Security would then reduce his survivor's benefit by that amount, so he would then receive about $1,050 ($2,300 less $1,250) as a Social Security survivor's benefit - assuming he is at FRA.

Although his $1,900 police pension will continue, he would see a big and immediate drop ($4,200 combined income from both spouses reduced to $2,950) in his household income. Would his monthly expenses drop by 30%? Probably not.

The popular press will tell you that most retirees do not need life insurance (except for perhaps final expenses or estate planning for the very wealthy). I beg to differ. I deal with real people and their incomes – many of them will be put in a very precarious financial position with the loss of all or much of one spouse's monthly retirement income.

Here's an example of GPO for spousal benefits. If Lee Ann worked in a job that did not pay into Social Security, her spousal benefit will be subject to the Government Pension Offset and be reduced by two-thirds of the amount of her own government pension.

In this case, Lyle's PIA is $2,200 and Lee Ann receives a teacher's pension of $2,100. If Lee Ann files for her spousal benefit at her FRA, her $1,100 spousal benefit (50% of Lyle's PIA) would be reduced by $1,400 (2/3 of her own government pension), bringing it down to zero due to GPO. She would get no Social Security benefits. Her survivor's benefit would just be $800. IF... her pension was only $900/month instead, her 50% spousal benefit of $1,100 would be cut by $600 (2/3 of $900) bringing it down to just $500 and survivors benefit to $1,600.

Social Security Strategies to Maximize Lifetime Income

Soon-to-be Social Security recipients don't often realize they can receive more income or adjust that stream of income to meet their needs by choosing one strategy over another. Did you know that the official Social Security Handbook has more than 2,700 separate rules governing the program's benefits?

The Social Security Administration's official website offers good information and some retirement calculators, but it doesn't offer software to really show the range of financial goals that individuals and couples can select. For example, married couples may want to maximize cumulative benefits as a "couple" or perhaps they might like to minimize the immediate drop in income for the surviving spouse. The same applies to surviving spouses and divorced spouses. Singles can choose the best way to achieve various income goals as well.

I use very interactive commercial Social Security software to show my own clients various planning strategies and how they maximize short-term or lifetime income goals by taking early benefits, delaying – with varying or without inflations assumptions. The visual results make it easy for me to share and you to see (and understand) 100's of your various planning options with a few touches of the button.

In any case, I think that I have made the case throughout this book, that if you (or your spouse) are very healthy and you are likely to live beyond age 80 or so, you should seriously consider delaying starting your Social Security benefits for as long as possible to receive the greatest amount of lifetime benefits (and survivor) available to you. In addition to getting much larger checks, one might realize several tax-saving advantages that will be discussed further later on.

Of course for many people, that is just not possible, feasible... or even the "right" decision to make. Perhaps your health is not so good or your family history for a long life is not on your side. Maybe you are out of work at age 62 (forced to retire, laid off, etc.) and have no viable employment prospects, so forgoing an immediate income from Social Security doesn't make any sense given your current circumstances. There are no black and white "best decisions".

There was a life expectancy chart earlier in the book that is helpful but 50% of the people will live longer and the other half shorter than that chart shows. Which half will you be in? Which half will your spouse be in?

Another good resource to check is **www.livingto100.com** There are others like it on the web too. They all ask personal health, diet, and lifestyle along with family history questions (anonymously) and then give you a more personalized educated "guess" about your life expectancy based on your answers. However, none of the websites take into account the continuous stream of wonderful medical advances to keep us alive and healthier longer. And at the end of the day, it's still just a more personalized "guess" – nothing more.

If you have already taken early Social Security (and received more than 12 months of checks) and are now having second thoughts about that decision... or perhaps your circumstances have changed, you can wait until your FRA and then voluntarily suspend your checks. There is no payback of those benefits! But each year that you suspend, your current benefit will grow by the 8% delayed credits (up until age 70) plus any COLA's. However, the 8% growth will not be on your PIA, but on your actual early benefits that you are receiving. This would also increase a survivor's benefit as well.

And while I'm on the subject of fixing a filing mistake, if you have received Social Security benefits for less than one year, you have the option to repay all of that income (without any interest) and you get a "do-over" as if you never filed at all. That may be a great option for you to consider, in order to take full advantage of the information coming up next in this book. Paying back these benefits might just be the best "investment" you'll ever make.

So before we discuss more "advanced" Social Security planning strategies, let's circle back around to the most basic decisions of when to apply and begin receiving your monthly benefits. Earlier we discussed the "penalties" for taking early Social Security and the "carrots" for delaying it.

Let's talk about more "breakeven" ages. In other words, how many years do you have to live to get more cumulative dollars if you delay taking benefits? We'll look at three scenarios as an example.

In the breakeven analysis, we think in terms of monthly income that you will spend to help pay for your retirement lifestyle. After that we'll delve into the concept of "investing" your checks if you don't need the income right away. Since many of my wealthier clients do not need the monthly income from Social Security, the question they often ask me is what might be the right decision if they turned around and invested each of those checks given assumed returns (which are not guaranteed).

Why would someone do that? Perhaps you want to get every dollar that you can out of the program if you don't live as long as you think or if Social Security goes "broke" or changes the rules, etc.).

"Breakeven" Analysis

Most financial planners talk about breakeven ages without taking into account the beneficial effects of COLA's (at least in terms your monthly check increasing over time). In my opinion, that is a mistake. But this will help you grasp the concept. From there we can look at breakeven with some inflation protection included (COLAs).

Twin sisters Donna and Theresa both have the same PIA of $2,000 at FRA at age 66. Donna decides to take early Social Security at age 62 so her monthly check will be $1,500 (a 25% haircut). By taking early benefits, Donna will get 48 more monthly checks than Theresa (who will wait to start benefits at FRA and get the full $2,000).

By starting benefits early, Donna will get $72,000 ($1,500 x 48 months) before Theresa gets her first check. So how long will it take Theresa's $500 larger check to catch-up? Well we simply need to divide $72,000 by $500 and we'll see that it is 144 months or a dozen years. Therefore the breakeven age is 78 (66 plus the 12 years). From then on, Theresa will be much better off by $500 a month for the rest of her life. Keep in mind that these figures ignore potential COLA's.

To go back to the life expectancy table, 62 year old females have a life expectancy of 84.5 years. So if Theresa just lives to her life expectancy, she will collect 12.5 years (from age 66 to 84.5) of larger checks than Donna... about $75,000 ($500 x 150 months). But the difference could be much, much greater.

When you add in the high likelihood of COLA's (cost of living adjustments) to those annual incomes, the cumulative difference could easily be TWICE as much as $75,000 through her life expectancy (depending upon the size and frequency of the annual COLA's).

COLA's would also lower the breakeven age. This makes logical sense since the arbitrary 2.8% is applied equally to the lower or higher amounts. A 2.8% increase on $1,500 is $42, while 2.8% on $2,000 is $56. So the larger amount will grow faster and faster over time.

Here is another example showing three different people aged 62, who all have earned the maximum Social Security earnings throughout their career so they all have the SAME PIA of $2,230. We will arbitrarily assume an annual COLA increase of 2.8%. COLA's could be more, less or zero some years, but this is just a simple illustration to make the point. Let's add COLA's to the next example.

Joe will retire at 62 so his monthly check will be $1,672. Lyle will retire at FRA (66) with a COLA-adjusted monthly income of $2,490.

Why is Lyle's amount more than his PIA? Because while he is waiting to start receiving benefits, his PIA will still increase with COLA's during those four years. Lyle will be four years and about $84,000 behind Joe in getting checks. But as you will see in a moment, it won't take Lyle long to catch-up and hit breakeven on a cumulative basis.

Jo Ann decides to wait until age 70 to begin taking benefits so she can earn delayed credits as well as COLA adjustments on a larger amount. So her first check with these assumptions would be $3,672. That's more than twice as large as Joe's check – but Joe will get 8 more years (96 months) of payments before Jo Ann gets her first check.

So let's compare ages when the cumulative Social Security checks (including COLA's) will be more or less equal assuming a constant 2.8% COLA and the same exact PIA's and birth years for all three retirees.

At age 75, Joe has collected some $338,000 in benefits from age 62. Lyle will have received $339,000 or so in benefits at age 75 even though his Social Security income began four years later.

Now Jo Ann will have to wait until she is 76 to have nearly as much cumulative benefits ($335,000) as the other fellows. By age 78, she will have received more benefits than Joe ($444,000 vs. $429,000) despite the fact that Joe began his income stream 8 years earlier.

And by the time all three retirees are age 80, Jo Ann's lifetime Social Security income will have eclipsed them all. At that point Joe has received $494,000, Lyle has gotten $547,000 and Jo Ann has enjoyed $558,000. From there on... the differences get wider and wider.

Remember that all of their life expectancies are over age 80. The men should live to about age 81 and she should live to 83.5. If they all live to age 87, Joe will get $40,017 that year, Lyle will get $53,362 and Jo Ann will get $70,461. Those are some big income differences.

And just for fun, if they all live to age 92, Joe will have received $970,000, Lyle will have gotten $1,182,000 and Jo Ann will have laughed all the way to the bank with over $1,396,000 in total benefits. Jo Ann will have received over $425,000 more than Joe. That's a serious difference.

Again, everyone's circumstances, health, family history and lifestyle are different, but it certainly would be foolish for most folks to completely ignore the foregoing when making your own decisions regarding when to begin your Social Security benefits.

Now you won't be comparing benefits to two other people like we did above. You will be comparing your own benefits to 1) taking early retirement, 2) waiting for your FRA or 3) earning delayed credits up to age 70 and everything in between. There are 96 months from age 62 through 70 to begin benefits and each month of delay adds to your income. Each month of delay means a higher monthly check.

Keep in mind that if you are married and have the higher earnings record, that your decision will not only affect you during your lifetime, but it can have profound implications on your surviving spouse. As a professional planner, I think that is very important to remember.

Most people can see the potential advantages of waiting until FRA or beyond to begin collecting benefits (assuming you don't get hit by a bus before breakeven), but still want to... or have to retire early for any number of reasons. There is still some savvy retirement planning that might be done – especially if you have other assets that might be used to fill the income gap while you delay starting Social Security.

That is when a retirement income planner specialist can be of great assistance. They can take a hard look at your assets, other income (pensions, interest, etc.) and complete financial situation and can oftentimes come up with a plan for you to be able to retire now... while delaying Social Security.

Investing Your Monthly Social Security Checks

For most readers, this section will not be meaningful as they will depend on Social Security checks to help meet their retirement lifestyle goals – otherwise known as paying the monthly bills. And much of the following discussion is completely dependent upon which rate of return you assume that you will earn over two or three decades of investing your monthly checks as well as the COLA increases (we assume it's a static 2.8% here).

Again, the point of these next paragraphs is to compare taking early benefits (age 62) and investing those at "X" percentage assumed annual return... to waiting until age 70 (earning delayed credits) and then doing the same thing with a much larger monthly check. It's a logical conclusion that the higher rate of return that you can earn, the higher the breakeven age (of delaying benefits until 70) would be.

If invested benefits (pre-tax) are invested at an average of 4%, the breakeven age is 81. That means that after that age (81) you would have more money if you wait and earn delayed credits at age 70.

An investor who can consistently earn 6% a year with his monthly benefit checks, the breakeven point rises to age 84. And for those few investors who consistently earn 8%, you would have to live to age 90 to be better off with delayed credits.

Let's put some numbers to both extremes – 4% at the low end and 8% at the higher end. Assume an initial Social Security annual income at age 62 of $20,064 with COLA's of 2.8% for both of them.

In this scenario, delayed credits and COLA's at age 70, would give an annual delayed Social Security income of $44,052.

Ellen takes early Social security at 62 and by age 69 (under the above assumptions) she has enjoyed an account balance (total income) of $211,000 before Linda has even received a single check. Although Linda's total first years payments at age 70 are $44,052, she has a lot of catching up to do. Ellen's Social Security income that same year is only $25,000.

At age 80, Ellen has some $724,000 in her account while Linda's balance has almost caught up with $704,000. The following year with a Social Security income of almost double Ellen's, Linda's account balance surpasses Ellen's and Linda's balance will grow disproportionally larger every year thereafter. At age 90, Ellen's account has grown to over $1,549,000 while Linda's total income from Social Security exceeds $1,881,000.

If both women could earn 8% over that same period, Ellen would have $251,000 before Linda even started collecting benefits. At this high earnings rate, it will take until age 90 for Linda's account to be slightly larger than Ellen's. Again, every year they live beyond that point, Linda's account grows faster due to her larger monthly checks (from the delayed credits).

But be honest with yourself. Do you really think that you can earn 8% year in and year out without taking too much risk? Bear in mind that the Social Security checks are guaranteed and presumably come with no risk, no stress or negative fluctuations. The checks keep coming during bear markets and recessions (there have been 23 recessions since 1900 – that's about one every 5-6 years).

And the other important point that you should carefully consider if you are married, is the survivor's benefit. That check will keep coming as long as even one of you is breathing.

Let me ask you something. What is missing from the foregoing discussion about investing your Social Security checks if you do not need the income for your lifestyle? The missing item is "income taxes". There was no accounting for potential (and very likely in this instance) federal income taxes on both your Social Security benefits... and your annual investment returns. Yes, most people in this financial position will be paying income taxes on up to 85% of the monthly benefits. And those 4%, 6% or 8% hypothetical earnings will get taxed each year along the way or at some point in the future.

Even if you avoid taxation on your monthly Social Security benefits (and wouldn't you likely have a lot of other income if you did not need to spend your monthly benefit check) and could put the proceeds into a tax-deferred annuity – but taxes will be due someday (upon eventual withdrawal or at death).

You could put the monthly benefit checks into a cash-value life insurance policy. If you did that, the death benefit would be both instantly increased (leveraged) and tax-free under longstanding laws. And a good policy will usually provide a net tax-free internal rate of return (IRR) at life expectancy of 5%-6% (after all policy loads, fees, expenses, etc.). But that tax-free return reduces slightly every year that you live beyond your expected lifespan.

The above discussion also assumes that one stops working at age 62 (or earns less than $15,720 per year). Otherwise the checks would be withheld ($1 withheld for every $2 earned over that amount) and therefore not be able to be invested and benefit from compounding.

So when you add potential taxation to the equation of investing your monthly checks into a taxable account, you might come up with a different answer unless you can reliably count on very high average returns in tax-advantaged investments. For most folks, my general advice would be to delay benefits and earn 8% guaranteed credits rather than try and "beat the game" by investing those early checks.

Let's continue looking at other ways that couples can maximize their combined Social Security benefits. Earlier in this book, I mentioned the file and suspend strategy and gave a short example, but let's take a closer look at this little-known income strategy.

As powerful as this strategy may be for many couples, it is my understanding that fewer than 2% of all couples actually take advantage of this way to add $10,000's to their overall lifetime benefits.

File and Suspend

As mentioned a few times before in this book, Congress passed a law in November of 2015 which substantially changed the rules of "file and suspend" for most Americans. **Unless you turn age 66 on or before May 1, 2016 you will NOT be allowed to use this strategy**.

But if (and only if) you meet the NEW age requirements, this chapter will still be valid. As we've discussed throughout this book, a wife or husband is actually entitled to receive the higher of his or her own Social Security benefit (called the worker's benefit) or as much as fifty percent of what his or her spouse is entitled to receive at full retirement age (the spousal benefit).

But there was a catch under the Social Security rules. A wife or husband who is eligible to file for spousal benefits based on his or her spouse's record cannot do so <u>until</u> his or her spouse begins collecting their own retirement benefits. But there is an important exception known as file and suspend.

Under the former rules authorized by the Senior Citizens Freedom to Work Act of 2000, someone who has reached FRA but who doesn't want to begin collecting retirement benefits right away to take advantage of delayed credits, can decide to file their application for retirement benefits and then immediately request to have those benefits "suspended". When this happens, his or her eligible spouse can file for spousal benefits while the "worker's benefit" accrues delayed credits. (Now-only valid if you turn age 66 on or before May 1, 2016... AND actually files and suspends on or before April 30th, 2016).

The file and suspend benefit strategy is usually done when one spouse has much lower lifetime earning's record, and therefore will receive a higher monthly benefit based on his or her spouse's higher earnings record than on his or her own earnings record. But when the numbers are run, using real world COLA assumptions, the strategy can work in a variety of retirement situations.

Taking full advantage of this strategy can potentially raise lifetime retirement income in three important ways. First of all, the spouse with lower earnings can immediately claim a higher (spousal) benefit.

Secondly, the spouse with higher earnings who has suspended his or her benefits can capture and accrue delayed retirement credits at a rate of 8% per year up until the age of 70 to increase his or her monthly retirement benefit by as much as 32%.

And finally, the surviving spouse's benefit which is available to the lower-earning spouse will also increase because a surviving spouse (at their FRA) will receive a benefit equal to 100% of the monthly retirement benefit the other spouse was receiving (or was entitled to receive) at the time of his or her death.

Now it is true that at the higher earning spouse's death there will be only one retirement benefit check a month instead of two. But that check will be based on a much higher earnings record along with the huge benefit of delayed credits. Let's look at an example.

Jason is a piano salesman who is about to reach his full retirement age of 66, but he wants to delay filing for Social Security benefits so that he can increase his monthly benefit from $2,250 at full retirement age (his PIA) to $2,970 at age 70 which is 32% more.

His wife Carol (who has had substantially lower lifetime earnings so her PIA is just $800) wants to retire in a few months at her full retirement age which is also age 66. With Jason's PIA of $2,250 and her own PIA of $800, at FRA Carol will be eligible for a higher monthly spousal benefit based on Jason's larger earning's record rather than on her own PIA. Of course if she wants benefits before her FRA, both the spousal and her own benefits would be reduced as discussed earlier.

Carol can receive the substantially higher spousal benefit (50% of Jason's $2,250 PIA) as soon as she retires at FRA or $1,125 a month instead of her own $800 benefit. But first, Jason must file an application for his own benefits, and then immediately suspend the benefits so he can then earn delayed retirement credits.

In actual fact, Carol will get her own benefit of $800 but that figure will be adjusted upward by $325 to reflect her spousal benefit of 50% of Jason's PIA. Could Jason have foregone the file and suspend strategy and still accrued delayed credits? Of course he could!

But then Carol could not have filed for the larger spousal benefit (as the higher earning spouse must have filed for benefits for the spousal benefit to be available). So without Jason's having employed the file and suspend strategy, Carol would have been limited to her own PIA of $800 (at FRA) until Jason actually filed for his own benefits.

If Jason had waited until age 70 to do so (to gain maximum delayed credits), then Carol would have lost out on four years of the additional $325 a month payments. That would have cost her $15,600 of total benefits over just those four years.

And can you imagine if Carol had no earnings history of her own, (no PIA) but Jason still wanted to accrue delayed credits to age 70? If they didn't know about file and suspend, she could not get her spousal benefits until Jason filed at age 70. That would have been a $54,000 mistake (losing out on 48 months of $1,125 monthly – plus COLA's) while Jason was earning delayed credits to benefit them both while he is alive... and presumably for her as a survivor's benefit.

So why did less than 2% of couples use this powerful strategy? Because so few people know about it or had a financial advisor walk them through the conversation of a lifetime of increased benefits (and the potential for you to change your mind if circumstances change).

*** If you file and suspend and change your mind later (perhaps your spouse has passed on or your health has changed), you can actually get a lump sum payment for all of those past month checks that you suspended. So in effect, you got a do-over. Very few people know this lump sum rule existed – but it goes away with the new law for those who do not file and suspend on or prior to April 30th, 2016.

File and suspend may or may not be the right strategy for you to use, but there are a few other little-known strategies to get full advantage of all of your contributions (FICA taxes) to Social Security.

Get some income now... and get even MORE later...

This next rule has is also in the process of being eliminated by the new law. But there is a much longer window of opportunity to take advantage of it. **As long as you turn age 62 (or older) sometime during the year 2015, you can still take advantage of this when you reach full retirement age (FRA).** Specifically, for Social Security purposes, you will be age 62 if your actual birthday is on or before Jan. 1, 1954. If you do not meet this age test, you can skip this chapter.

This other advanced Social Security strategy can be used to increase household income for retirees. The idea here is to have one spouse file for spousal benefits first, and then switch to his or her own higher retirement benefit later with delayed credits.

Once a spouse reaches their full retirement age (FRA) and is eligible for a spousal benefit based on his or her spouse's earnings record (PIA), he or she can choose to file a "restricted" application for spousal benefits, while delaying applying for their own retirement benefits based on his or her own earnings record (their PIA) in order to earn 8% delayed retirement credits.

Let's look at an example of this strategy in action. Meredith files for her Social Security retirement benefit of $2,450 per month at age 66 (based on her own earning's record). Her husband Doug wants to wait until age 70 to file and benefit from delayed credits. At his full retirement of age 66 Doug applies for spousal benefits (while restricting his own benefits) based on Meredith's earnings record (since she has already filed for her own retirement benefits)

Since Doug receives 50% of Meredith's PIA ($1,225 per month) right now (while she is getting her full PIA now as well). He can delay applying for retirement benefits based on his own earnings record (which is $2,466 per month PIA at full retirement age) so that he can earn 8% delayed retirement credits and increased COLA's.

At age 70 Doug will switch from collecting a spousal benefit to his own larger worker's retirement benefit of $4,060 per month (32% higher than his PIA at age 66… plus COLA's assumed at 2.8% per year).

There are many benefits to this strategy since it not only increases their combined household income right now, but it also enables Meredith to receive a much larger survivor's benefit in the event of Doug's death.

As mentioned above, this "Restricted" application strategy can be used in a variety of scenarios, but the above example illustrates how it might be used when both spouses have substantial earning's records and similar PIA's but they do not want to postpone one's applying for benefits to earn delayed credits. But similar PIA's are not necessary for a "restricted" application to add to a couple's retirement income. Let's look at the next example.

Nelly and Josh want to get as much Social Security retirement income now as possible, but benefit from Josh's delayed credits too. They are both at full retirement age (FRA) although Josh wants to continue working at his business. Josh's PIA is $2,000 and Nelly's is $800. First, Nelly files for benefits based on her own earning's record and Josh files a restricted application for spousal benefits so his own benefits will earn delayed credits. Being at FRA, Josh's income from his business will not affect his Social Security benefits.

So Nelly gets her $800 PIA and Josh gets the 50% spousal benefit of $400. By doing this Josh will get a larger benefit at age 70 and Nelly will get a larger potential survivor's benefit should she outlive Josh. In the intervening 4 years, while Josh waits for age 70, he will have gotten over $19,200 in spousal benefits (48 months x $400). When he turns 70 he will get his own benefit of $2,640 (plus COLA's) and drop the spousal benefit.

But it gets even better. Since Nelly waited until her FRA, she can and will drop her own $800 benefit and take her spousal benefit based on Josh's $2,000 PIA. So her monthly check will increase to $1,000 (plus COLA's) when Josh claims his own benefit. Very smart!

Each and every couple's circumstances are unique, and these advanced claiming strategies may not be appropriate for everyone.

When deciding when and how to apply for Social Security benefits, one must make sure they consider a number of claiming strategies that take into account one's financial situation as well as factors such as both spouses' ages, estimated benefits and their life expectancies.

The 62/70 Strategy

Many married couples cannot afford to postpone collecting Social Security while waiting for each to turn age 70 and both enjoy delayed credits. When we can delay at least one person's collecting (by using other assets to fill in for that monthly check), we can use a simple technique known as the "62/70 Strategy". This strategy can maximize benefits over the long term.

With this claiming system, the lower-earning spouse files for Social Security at age 62 and the higher earner delays until age 70. By doing it this way, no matter which spouse passes away first, the smaller monthly benefit will drop off and the higher one will remain. This basic part of claiming strategy is NOT affected by the new laws.

For this example, let's assume Todd's full benefit (PIA) will be $1,850 a month. His wife Lisa's full retirement benefit will be $1,162 a month - so at 62, she'd receive $871 a month (75% of $1,162). Lisa applies for her $871 benefit at 62 while Todd delays claiming his own benefit until age 70. By delaying his own benefits they will grow by 32% when he'll collect $2,442.

Should Todd die before Lisa, his monthly benefit will then become Lisa's survivor benefit, and it will be much higher than Lisa would have received if Todd had begun collecting at age 62. If Todd outlives Lisa, her smaller check will drop off and he will continue to get his own larger check than he would have gotten if he claimed for early benefits like Lisa did.

But if you've paid attention, I am guessing that you have already figured out how to make the above scenario even better for Todd and Lisa (assuming Todd was 62 or older before January 1st 1954). Couples should always take advantage of all of the little-known rules to increase their Social Security retirement income.

Going back to Todd and Lisa, let's give their retirement income another boost. Although Todd is waiting until 70 to start receiving his benefits, at 66 (FRA) he can apply for the 50% "restricted" spousal benefit based on Lisa's PIA while his own benefit keeps growing. Of course he must be at full retirement age in order to do this.

Because he has reached FRA (and born on or before January 1st, 1954 under the new law), Todd qualifies for the maximum spousal benefit (50%): $581 a month which is half of Lisa's $1,162 PIA. When Todd turns 70, he'll replace the spousal benefit and start collecting his own larger benefit with four years of 8% delayed credits.

By adding this twist (filing a restricted application), the household added $27,888 of Social Security income ($581 X 48 months – excluding COLA's) while still benefiting from the fact that as long as either of them live, the larger check will continue.

Filing a restricted application is like "double dipping". Not the double dipping strategy that happens when government workers who retire from one job and then go back to work elsewhere (or sometimes exactly where they "left" as a consultant). Social Security double dipping refers to the ability to draw your spousal benefit and your regular benefit (based on your own PIA) at different points during your retirement (again, only if you are age 62 or older in 2015).

To implement the "restricted application" strategy, you must specifically file for the spousal benefit when you file, so make sure this is clearly stated on your application. It's VERY important to remember that if you are eligible for both a spousal benefit and your regular benefit and did not turn age 62 in 2015, the Social Security Administration will deem that you are filing for both benefits when you file, and it will simply give you the higher of the two.

If you don't file in the correct manner, you will not be able to change your election years down the road when you discover your mistake. Since you can only draw one benefit at a time, it may make sense to take your spousal benefit (even if it's lower) for a few years and then switch to your own benefit later on with delayed credits.

Why would this possibly be a financially sound idea? Here's an example. When Katie reaches her full retirement age, she can either file for her own benefit of $1,200 per month or her spousal benefit of $1,150 per month. On the surface it would seem like a pretty easy decision to choose her own higher benefit of $1,200, wouldn't it?

But don't forget that your own monthly benefit amount will grow by 8% a year if you delay taking it until age 70. In Katie's case, her regular benefit would grow by 32% to $1,584 per month if she delays taking it until she turns 70. By accepting a smaller benefit for a few years, she would receive a much larger benefit for the rest of her life.

You see that her own benefit will grow while her 50% spousal (or divorced) benefit will not (if we exclude COLA's which will grow both benefits). But COLA's on $1,584 will grow her monthly benefit much more than the same COLA's on her $1,150 spousal benefit.

When all is said and done, the most important thing that couples can do when making their Social Security claiming decisions is to look at all options by running the numbers (with COLA assumptions too) and make those very serious decisions based on all of their financial circumstances, goals, risk tolerance, health, life expectancy, etc.

Can you delay one or both checks in order to maximize your lifetime Social Security income? Can you, with the help of a financial advisor, plan for other income from your assets so that you can retire when you want to, but still benefit from larger lifetime Social Security checks which are guaranteed and likely to grow with COLA's?

I submit to you, that whatever you ultimately decide to do, you should at the very least, carefully examine all financial alternatives with a financial professional that has a lot of experience with BOTH Social Security claiming strategies as well as retirement income planning. You always should dig deeper than your first best guess.

Some Income Tax Planning Strategies

Right along with "filing" strategies... are income tax strategies which, in the right circumstances can substantially lower your retirement income taxes over your lifetime. And when we can reduce your tax burden, we simultaneously increase your net spendable income. And everyone loves to reduce their tax bill!

Oftentimes in my practice I come across a couple who are adamant about retiring early – sometimes right at age 62 or sometime before their FRA. And if you can afford to do that, that's wonderful.

But for many folks who would like to do this, they feel they must begin taking Social Security income right away so they don't deplete their other savings too quickly. And that may be the case. But along with taking advantage of filing strategies, most people should look at potential (and very substantial) tax saving strategies.

These tax savings can add up to a bundle over 10, 20 or 30 years as you will see shortly.

Back in the section about taxation, I discussed how IRA's, 401K's and 403B's etc. are taxed differently than Social Security. The former are fully taxed (100% of all dollars) as funds are withdrawn while in the worst case, at least 15% of your Social Security dollars are tax-free – and maybe much more.

You may also remember that only 50% of your Social Security benefits are included in determining your provisional income (how much of your Social Security check is taxable). Again the provisional income formula is your adjusted gross income plus 50% of your Social Security benefits plus tax-exempt interest (from muni-bonds). But 100% of IRA dollars are used in that same calculation. Interesting!

So if one thinks about this logically, you might be able to take twice as many Social Security dollars for income than income from an IRA – without paying more taxes to the IRS. Would it make sense to think that $1,000 from Social Security might be worth more than $1,000 from your IRA? Has anyone, including your CPA, ever taught you about this?

One more thing – state income taxes. Depending on where you live you might have to pay state income taxes on Social Security.

Right now thirteen states with broad-based income taxes do tax Social Security to some extent: six states (Minnesota, Nebraska, North Dakota, Rhode Island, Vermont and West Virginia) generally tax Social Security income to the same extent that it is taxed by the IRS.

Another four states (Connecticut, Kansas, and Montana) generally tax a smaller fraction of Social Security income than the IRS does. Kansas residents can exclude Social Security income if their adjusted gross income is less than $75,000.

Three other states (Colorado, New Mexico and Utah) require that federally untaxed Social Security benefits be added back to federal AGI to calculate the base against which their own broad age-determined income exclusions apply.

If you live in one of the above states, the following discussion might even be more appealing. Either way, taxation is always something to think about and consider when making virtually irreversible (with few exceptions) Social Security benefit decisions.

Again, this strategy is not going to be applicable for everyone. But if by using a smart filing strategy (delaying your benefits) to dramatically increase your Social Security income for the rest of your life and enjoying larger annual COLA increases (in actual dollars)... while reducing future taxable income, would that be a retirement strategy worth exploring?

I have copied the taxation of Social Security chart here for your easy reference so you don't have to flip back through the pages.

Taxation of Social Security benefits

Your Tax Filing Status	Provisional Income**	Amount of Social Security benefits that are subject to any taxation (I.R.S.)
Married filing jointly	Under $32,000	0%
	$32,000 - $44,000	Up to 50%
	Over $44,000	Up to 85%
Single, head of household, qualifying widow(er), married filing separately and living apart from spouse	Under $25,000	0%
	$25,000 - $34,000	Up to 50%
	Over $34,000	Up to 85%
Married - filing separately and living with spouse	Over $0	85%

Provisional Income = AGI PLUS one-half of your SS benefit(s) PLUS all tax-exempt interest (muni bonds)

So let's explore this strategy a little more by looking at two couples who choose to file in different ways. We'll first look at the Earlys and then the Waites. After that we'll take a look at the Bests who use some advanced retirement income planning strategies along with savvy Social Security filing to dramatically cut their long-term taxable income – and keep more cash in their pocket for their lifestyle.

For all of the couples, let's make this very simple to highlight how taxation can affect the filing decisions that you might make. All couples have $34,000 of Social Security income and have a goal of $80,000 income (before taxes) to enjoy the lifestyle they want in retirement. **But the income tax bill for each couple will be different!**

The Earlys and the Waites have traditional IRA's that they have rolled over from 401(k)'s at their previous jobs. They have no muni-bond interest and we will exclude personal exemptions, tax deductions, etc. to focus in on this specific taxation discussion.

First, let's compute the provisional income of the Earlys who have decided to begin Social Security at age 62 in order to not deplete their IRA funds so quickly since they will need lower IRA distributions ($34,000) than the Waites to get the pre-tax income goal of $80,000.

They get $34,000 from Social Security, so we'll include 50% of that figure to calculate provisional income. Since we'll need $46,000 of IRA distributions to reach the goal of $80,000 pre-tax ($34,000 of Social Security plus $46,000 from IRA's), let's see how this looks:

$17,000	(50% of Social Security $34,000 income)
+$46,000	100% of IRA distributions
$63,000	Provisional income

Let's compute the amount of Social Security taxable income now.

$63,000	Provisional income
- $32,000	first threshold for couple filing jointly (see above chart)
$31,000	amount over $32,000 first threshold
x 50%	to determine how much over the 1st threshold is subject
$15,500	to taxation

Now let's compute the amount over the second threshold to find the total amount of Social Security income that is subject to taxation at their marginal tax rate.

$63,000	Provisional income
- $44,000	second threshold for couple filing jointly (see above chart)
$19,000	amount over $44,000 first threshold

<u>x   35%</u>   to determine how much of the 2nd threshold is subject
$ 6,650   to taxation

When we add the amounts subject to taxation from the amounts over the first ($15,500) and second thresholds ($6,650), we get a total of $22,150 Social Security that is subject to taxation.

Next we add in the $46,000 of IRA distributions to the taxable Social Security amount of $22,150 that they need to reach the pre-tax income goal of $80,000 and we get a grand total of $66,150 TOTAL taxable income.

Now let's look at the Waites situation. Since they waited to begin taking Social Security, their Social Security income is $58,000. Because their Social Security income is so much larger, they only need to take $22,000 out of their IRA's to reach the same $80,000 pre-tax income goal.

Before we do the same computation as we just did for the Earlys, let me address a major issue here – assuming the Waites stopped working at the same age as the Earlys. That elephant in the room is where did they get the $80,000 a year to live on while they were delaying Social Security?

Well we have to assume in the absence of a paycheck that it came from IRA distributions. If the Waites had to take 8 years of $80,000 IRA distributions in order to retire early, then obviously they are depleting their IRA's faster than the Earlys who only needed to take $46,000 a year out. We'll explore this further in a few moments.

The Waites get $58,000 from Social Security, so we'll include 50% of that figure ($29,000) to calculate provisional income. Since we'll need $22,000 of IRA distributions to reach the goal of $80,000 pre-tax ($34,000 of Social Security plus $46,000 from IRA's), let's see how this looks:

$29,000 (50% of Social Security $58,000 income)
<u>+$22,000</u> 100% of IRA distributions
$51,000 Provisional income

Let's compute the amount of Social Security taxable income now.

```
 $51,000   Provisional income
- $32,000   first threshold for couple filing jointly (see above chart)
 $19,000   amount over $32,000 first threshold
x     50%   to determine how much over the 1st threshold is subject
 $ 9,500        to taxation
```

Now let's compute the amount over the second threshold to find the total amount of Social Security income that is subject to taxation at their marginal tax rate.

```
 $51,000   Provisional income
- $44,000   second threshold for couple filing jointly (see above chart)
 $ 7,000   amount over $44,000 first threshold
x     35%   to determine how much of the 2nd threshold is subject
 $ 2,450        to taxation
```

When we add the amounts subject to taxation from the amounts over the first threshold ($9,500) and second threshold ($2,450), we get a total of $11,950 Social Security that is subject to taxation.

Next we add in the $22,000 of IRA distributions to the taxable Social Security amount of $11,950 that the Waites need to reach their pre-tax income goal of $80,000 and we get a grand total of $33,950 TOTAL taxable income.

That's just over half of the Earlys taxable income. Only 21% of the Waites $58,000 Social Security is subject to income tax. Compare that low taxable percentage of benefits to the Earlys -- 65% of their $34,000 Social Security income that would be subject to taxation.

Who says that a thousand dollars from Social Security is worth the same as a thousand dollars from an IRA? Someone with an advisor who has never done the calculation for them.

So at this point in time, despite both couples having the same pre-tax income of $80,000 the Waites have a much lower amount of taxable income ($33,950) than the Earlys ($66,150) and therefore would pay the IRS much less in taxes. At the 15% marginal tax bracket, the Waites will pay $4,830 LESS in annual taxes to the IRS.

But we still have to look at the total situation, because the Earlys depleted much less of their IRA's for the first number of years in order to gain a much larger Social Security income. Excluding (COLAs) and all other tax-related issues let's see how their taxable incomes compare over their retirements. We'll get to the Bests in a moment.

Age	The Earlys	The Waites	The Bests
	Taxable Incomes For Each Couple		
62	$66,150	$80,000	$72,000
63	$66,150	$80,000	$72,000
64	$66,150	$80,000	$72,000
65	$66,150	$80,000	$72,000
66	$66,150	$80,000	$72,000
67	$66,150	$80,000	$72,000
68	$66,150	$80,000	$72,000
69	$66,150	$80,000	$72,000
70	$66,150	$33,950	$17,500
71	$66,150	$33,950	$17,500
72	$66,150	$33,950	$17,500
73	$66,150	$33,950	$17,500
73	$66,150	$33,950	$17,500
74	$66,150	$33,950	$17,500
75	$66,150	$33,950	$17,500
76	$66,150	$33,950	$17,500
77	$66,150	$33,950	$17,500
78	$66,150	$33,950	$17,500
79	$66,150	$33,950	$17,500
80	$66,150	$33,950	$17,500
81	$66,150	$33,950	$17,500
82+	and so on thereafter until the loss of one (the smallest) Social Security check at the passing of the first spouse.		

Although the Waites have almost $14,000 more taxable income in the first few years (in this case 8 years), they have about half of the taxable income once they turn on their Social Security income stream and for as long as they both live.

And another point which is not included here is that the COLA's on the Waites income will grow that income much faster than the Earlys. Over time, even at 2-2.5% average COLA's will add up to many $1,000's of extra (low-taxed) income.

The same logic would hold true for a single person, as provisional income only counts 50% of Social Security dollars and unlike IRA income, at least 15% of Social Security dollars will be tax free.

As discussed earlier in this book, if one (or your spouse) does not live to life expectancy, they may be better off taking early. If we exclude COLA's (which are unknown and not guaranteed... but historically very likely) the actuarial comparison between taking early Social Security and delaying are equal if you live to life expectancy.

Now, it can be said that the Waites are taking more investment risks since they are taking more money out of their IRA's sooner. But there are many financial planning strategies and products that can almost eliminate or greatly reduce that risk. I'll highlight just one later.

However over the long term, since more income is provided to the Waites by Social Security, they may have much less investment risk over their entire retirement. You will recall that they are only needing $22,000 from their IRA's (after year 8) while the Earlys need to take more than double that amount ($46,000) every year for the rest of their lives.

Would you agree that Social Security income is probably more secure than an IRA? Would you also agree that increasing distributions by Social Security would be more likely than with an IRA – especially during and after a bad bear stock market or very low interest rates?

Again, everyone's situation is very different and the above discussion is meant to emphasize that income from Social Security is treated very differently than IRA income in our current tax code.

Who are the Bests? And what did they do differently?

Well the Bests, did some extra financial planning before retirement with an advisor that not only understood Social Security, but understands retirement income distributions and taxation. Like the Waites, the Bests also decide to delay taking income from Social Security and use other investments to make up the difference in their retirement income when they stopped working at age 62.

Earlier in this book I briefly mentioned how many of my personal clients use ROTH IRA's and cash value life insurance (where proper distributions are tax-free like a ROTH) to increase their net spendable income during retirement.

Most everyone understands that income from a ROTH is tax-free. Also mentioned earlier in the book was the fact that income from both a ROTH and a cash value life insurance policy does NOT count toward calculating provisional income (how much of your Social Security check will be subject to taxation). They are the only sources of regular income that are excluded from the calculation.

I won't go into specifics here as I basically wrote two books on using life insurance for a safe retirement income stream. I am not talking about "your father's" life insurance or even one that you probably own right now, but a unique, over-funded contract that is specifically designed for that purpose by an agent who really knows what they are doing.

But let's get back to the Bests. At some point along the line, perhaps years ago or perhaps at or during retirement, they made some savvy retirement income moves that put them in the position of reducing their taxable income in retirement even further than the Waites. They did this by either contributing to or to converting some traditional IRA's to a ROTH IRA.

Although a properly structured life contract can offer many more financial benefits than a ROTH IRA, as far as this discussion goes, we'll just focus on a ROTH IRA here since most of my readers are very familiar with them. But either one will net the same exact result.

Everything about the Bests is the same as the Waites – except that they can withdraw $8,000 a year from ROTH's instead of taking all $22,000 from their traditional IRA's. Again, we have to assume in the absence of a paycheck that it came from IRA distributions.

Similar to the Waites, the Bests have to take 8 years of $80,000 IRA distributions ($72,000 from traditional and $8,000 from a ROTH) in order to retire early. Therefore their taxable income is $8,000 less than the Waites... but just about $6,000 more than the Earlys in the first eight years of retirement.

Like the Waites, at age 70 the Bests get $58,000 from Social Security, so we'll include 50% of that figure ($29,000) to calculate provisional income. Since we'll need $14,000 of traditional IRA distributions and $8,000 from the ROTH to reach the goal of $80,000 pre-tax ($58,000 of Social Security plus $14,000 from traditional IRA's plus $8,000 from the ROTH), let's see how this looks:

```
 $29,000  (50% of Social Security $58,000 income)
+$14,000  100% of traditional IRA distributions
+     $0  (0% of $8,000 ROTH distributions count in the calculation)
 $43,000  Provisional income
```

Let's compute the amount of Social Security taxable income now.

```
 $43,000  Provisional income
-$32,000  first threshold for couple filing jointly (see above chart)
 $11,000  amount over $32,000 first threshold
x    50%  to determine how much over the 1st threshold is subject
$ 5,500        to taxation
```

Now let's compute the amount over the second threshold to find the total amount of Social Security income that is subject to taxation at their marginal tax rate. Please note: there is no overage here!

```
 $43,000  Provisional income
-$44,000  second threshold for couple filing jointly (see above chart)
$      0  amount over $44,000 first threshold
x    35%  to determine how much of the 2nd threshold is subject
$      0        to taxation
```

When we add the amounts subject to taxation from the amounts over the first threshold ($5,500) and second threshold ($0), we get a total of $5,500 Social Security that is subject to taxation.

Next we add in the $12,000 of traditional IRA distributions to the taxable Social Security amount of $5,500 that the Bests need to reach their pre-tax income goal of $80,000 and we get a grand total of $17,500 TOTAL taxable income. That's almost half of the Waites taxable income. Again, who says that a thousand dollars from Social Security is worth the same as a thousand dollars from an IRA?

In 2016, the first $18,550 of taxable income is taxed at only 10%, so all of their income is being taxed at only 10% instead of 15% by the IRS. Another real money advantage to planning ahead! On top of that, only 9% of their $58,000 Social Security income is subject to tax!

I cannot emphasis this enough. There are some real and very substantial retirement income planning opportunities when you take the time or hire a very knowledgeable and experienced financial advisor to help you make smart Social Security filing decisions.

Again, the foregoing is not meant to say that this is the "right" way to file for benefits. But has your stockbroker, banker, annuity salesperson, money manager or even your CPA discussed any of this with you? If they have, consider yourself fortunate. If they have not, perhaps you need to explore finding another financial advisor for your retirement. What other strategies might you be missing out on?

Because retirement income distribution is VERY different than retirement accumulation – which is what most of the above types of financial advisers spend their careers focusing on – a different skill-set is needed to maximize your spendable (after-tax) income. Focusing on SAFE income (withdrawals) is another big difference of attention, as opposed to focusing on trying to shoot for the fences to build savings.

To summarize the Social Security filing discussion for the previous sections of this book in a few words, would be to "know thy options"!

Make smart filing decisions based on all of the factors described in this book. Don't hesitate to get professional help. Even if you think the answer for you might be readily apparent and a no-brainer (and it might be), how else can you financially improve your retirement years by reducing risks and volatility, safely increasing your retirement income... or by reducing your tax burden?

I'll make a quick commercial here. I own both advanced (and know how to fully use) Social Security filing options software and taxation scenario software. As mentioned earlier in this book, only about 7% of financial advisers can honestly say that they are very competent in that specialized area. Of those advisers, even fewer feel very comfortable around tax planning scenarios.

Finally, my retirement clients look to me for SAFE money or even guaranteed retirement solutions. In other words, helping them manage their investments to avoid most of all stock, bond and other market risks (portfolio roller coaster rides) while getting good returns to beat inflation and not run out of money before you run out of life!

Feel free to contact me for a free, no-obligation telephone consultation. I am sure that you will be happy that you did.

Social Security Planning with Minor Children

I wasn't going to include a section on this topic because I thought that it would apply to so few people. But I was doing a Social Security income planning seminar at a local restaurant a few nights ago, and low and behold, an attendee and his wife asked me about it. So for the relatively few folks who will benefit from these next paragraphs, the extra, unplanned income could be substantial.

The gentleman and his wife told me that he was going to be 66 (FRA) in a few months and that she was ten years younger. They have two children still at home (and earning honor grades in high school) who are under the age of 18. They had heard that there might be some Social Security benefits for their minor children. Here's how it works.

Whether the children are natural, stepchildren or even legally adopted grandchildren who live at home and are under the age of 18 (or 19 if still in high school), the children can qualify for Social

Security benefits if the parent has filed for their own benefits at age 62 or older. In fact, this parent can EVEN file and suspend his/her benefit if still working full time or for whatever reason (even under the new laws if one is at FRA <u>before</u> May 2nd 2016) so that he can accrue delayed credits until age 70. Or just take the benefits early.

Each child can get 50% of his PIA until they turn 18. Assuming his PIA is $2,400 – each of the two kids can get $1,200 per month while he (in his own case) files and suspends his own benefits to earn delayed credits. That adds up to almost $50,000! Too bad that his wife is only 56 years old and is too young to claim her spousal benefit as well.

Believe it or not, even Donald Trump's minor children could qualify for benefits. Born in 1946, if he hasn't done so already, he could file and suspend his benefits and each minor child would be entitled to a pretty hefty monthly benefit until they reach age 18.

You should know that there is a family maximum benefit that Social Security will give under ANY circumstances. So the "old woman who lived in a shoe" kids would each get pro-rata lower benefits so as not to bring the family over the maximum allowed benefit.

Now if this gentleman who attended my seminar was 62 rather than 66, I would probably not recommend that he claim early Social Security (at the detriment to his own and his wife's long term Social Security income with COLA's) in order to get short term benefits for his kids. And since his wife is so much younger the reduced survivor benefit would make filing early an even bigger mistake. Not to mention that if he was still working at age 62, he would lose $1 of his own benefits for each $2 that he earned over $15,130.

Of course, the most common reason for children's benefits is for when a parent has died (no matter at what age as long as they had their 40 quarters) based on his PIA. There are many situations and rules regarding children's benefits and they are beyond the scope of this book. But after meeting this gentleman and his wife, I decided to add this not-so-common circumstance to the book.

Perhaps you may know somebody in this circumstance and might be able to pass along this basic information.

Social Security and Medicare

A full explanation of Medicare is beyond the scope of this book and my personal expertise. Medicare is not an area that my financial practice is directly involved with, but I am happy to give you a very basic summary here. "ObamaCare" may change the Medicare rules as well. You can get all of your questions answered by visiting the Social Security office nearest you, calling the Social Security Administration toll-free at 800-772-1213 or by visiting their website at www.ssa.gov or speak with an insurance agent that specializes in Medicare.

Gone are the good-ole days when Social Security and Medicare automatically went together and people would apply for them at the same point in time – at the age of 65.

Most everyone knows that the Social Security retirement age is increasing (for full retirement benefits), but normal Medicare can begin at age 65 (except in the event of disability and other circumstances).

So if you retire early – as early as age 62, you will have to wait for age 65 to begin Medicare coverage. And since you are likely not working if you have started Social Security, you will have to find individual health insurance (often with medical exams and full medical underwriting) which is going to be very expensive even if you are fortunate enough to enjoy good health.

However, if you want to delay beginning Social Security benefits to an age beyond 65 or whatever your full retirement age is, you can still apply for Medicare at age 65. This opportunity is especially attractive to those who have been paying for their health insurance premiums out of their own pocket, since Medicare Premiums (Part A and B) along with a good Medigap policy will likely cost less than they have been paying.

More than a few people are under the false impression that in order to apply for Medicare at age 65, that they have to have filed and be taking benefits from Social Security. As stated above, this is absolutely untrue. So where do your Part B premiums come from if there is no Social Security benefit to deduct the premiums from?

If you enroll in Medicare Part B before starting Social Security, the Centers for Medicare and Medicaid Services (CMS) will send you a quarterly bill for your Medicare premiums. You can pay these premiums by check or credit card. However, once you begin Social Security the Part B premiums must come out of your monthly Social Security check/deposit.

You should know that if you do not apply for Medicare in a timely manner, a 10% penalty (extra lifelong premium costs) may be added to your Part B Medicare premiums for each 12 month period that you have missed since becoming eligible.

Whether you have applied for Social Security retirement benefits or not, Medicare will mail your Medicare card three months before your 65th birthday. If your plan is to begin Social Security benefits at some point after you turn age 65, you have a seven month period of time (from 3 months prior to your 65th birthday and up to 4 months after it) to apply for Medicare health insurance benefits.

If you are going to continue being employed after age 65 and are covered by an employer group plan that covers 20 or more employees - or are covered as a spouse under such a plan - you do not have to enroll in Medicare at that point. Medicare coverage will begin when your current employer (or spouses) coverage stops and you apply for Medicare coverage.

In any case, you certainly do not want to have a gap in your health insurance coverage (be fully at financial risk) or be subject to any Medicare Part B penalties.

Basic Medicare has two parts: Part A and Part B. There is also Medicare Part C (privately insured Medicare Advantage Plans which combine Parts A and B – usually similar to an HMO) and Part D (prescription drug coverage). I will not be describing Part C and D in this book that is devoted to Social Security income benefits.

Part A is hospital insurance and helps pay for care in a hospital, home health care, hospice services and for skilled nursing home care (with a maximum of 100 days only). For those folks who are covered under Social Security and have paid into the Medicare system, there is no cost to be covered by Part A.

Before I continue, let me clear up one HUGE fallacy and that is that Medicare covers long-term care expenses. The truth is that Medicare covers very LITTLE long-term health care (LTC) costs. Virtually nothing!

Medicare care does NOT cover chronic custodial long term health costs in an assisted living facility or in a home setting. It will pay for limited and necessary "skilled" nursing services in a home setting for a condition that is going to get better (such as physical therapy after a stroke or broken hip). But not for a condition which is not going to get better.

Medicare does NOT pay benefits for chronic custodial physical problems (helping one bathe, dress, eat, toilet, transfer from a bed to a chair, etc.) or for cognitive issues such as Alzheimer's. For that type of coverage, one needs some type of private long term care insurance – typically referred to as a LTC policy.

Although I don't market LTC insurance much anymore, I actually began my financial services career as a LTC insurance specialist and I can tell you first hand of the importance of these types of policies. I tell everyone to find an LTC insurance specialist and look into getting this important coverage. Make sure they sell plans from <u>many</u> carriers.

I have my own LTC policy, my parents have theirs (one parent was on claim and received considerable monthly tax-free insurance benefits before she passed) and my brother and sister-in-law do too. I have had many of my LTC clients go on claim already over the years – with dozens more claims to come in the next decade or two.

Depending upon where you live in the country, long term care costs (home care, assisted living or nursing home expenses) can easily run $35,000-$95,000 per year. High out-of-pocket expenses for even just a few years can ruin many a retirement plan that did not plan for the high likelihood of someone needing expensive long term care.

A frequently cited statistic is that about 60% or more of all seniors will need long term care at some point in their lives. One in three people over age 85 are expected to get Alzheimer's. For some it will be for just a number of months, for others a few years and for a growing number of seniors with Alzheimers, five years or longer.

Even just $50,000 a year (about $4,200 per month), is enough to devastate most people's finances. If someone is single, what would that high level of "unplanned" monthly expense do to even the most carefully crafted retirement plans? It certainly would blow a major hole and perhaps a devastating blow to most monthly budgets and life savings. If you are married, it could have more severe financial consequences for the healthy spouse (usually the woman) as that person will have to live with the financial consequences.

Again, my main point here is just to let you know that Medicare does NOT really cover these long term care expenses and you should carefully think about how you and your family might financially deal with this likely occurrence and growing potential financial liability.

Getting back to Medicare, Part B covers medical insurance which helps pay for doctor's visits, preventative care, medical tests, outpatient care and some other medical services. Unlike Part A, the Part B premium is not free. The monthly Part B premium is deducted from your monthly Social Security check. Again, if you are not getting checks, the premium is billed quarterly.

For most retirees already getting Social Security checks, Part B costs $104.90 per month for each recipient (2016). For those who are on Medicare BUT NOT getting Social Security checks yet, the Part B premiums are $121.80 (2016). This difference is because of a 1987 "hold harmless" provision, which was designed to keep recipients' Social Security net checks from shrinking when Part B premiums rise but Social Security has no COLA that year.

That law provides that for ordinary retirees who have Part B premiums deducted from their Social Security checks, the standard premium <u>cannot</u> go up in any year by more than the extra dollars they're getting as a cost of living adjustment (COLA) in their Social Security checks. That protects 70% of recipients. Fair or not, the remaining 30% must pay ALL of the real increased costs of Part B.

There is also an annual out-of-pocket deductible of $166 for 2016 (inflation adjusted) plus 20% co-insurance. The 20% co-insurance means that unless you have a private Medigap policy (described in a moment), Medicare pays for 80% (after satisfying your deductible) and you pay 20% of your Medicare approved expenses out of your own pocket (up to a limit).

The monthly costs for Medicare Part B premiums are much higher for the "wealthy" with four more premium levels. **Having just $1 of income over the limit puts you into the next bracket and substantially increases each person's monthly premium.** For example, a couple with a Modified Adjusted Gross Income (MAGI) of $170,000 - $214,000 will pay a monthly premium of $170.50 (each). For a single tax filer, MAGI income of $85,000 - $107,000 will pay the same $170.50 monthly premium for 2016.

There are two premium levels in between, but the highest level of MAGI income for a couple (over $428,000) will pay $389.80 each in 2016 and a single filer needs just $214,000 of MAGI to "get" to pay that same highest monthly premium for Part B.

Selling a second home or rental property, selling an investment with large long-term capital gains or taking a bigger IRA distribution to help out a family member can cause your Part B premiums to soar.

Paying monthly Part B premiums are one thing, but a scarier potential issue is the 20% out-of-pocket co-pay. That potential devastating cost can be alleviated with what's called a Medigap policy.

A Medigap policy is a Medicare insurance supplement plan that is offered by private insurance companies. You may have seen the TV commercials or newspaper ads for these by AARP, United Health Care and many other for-profit insurance companies.

However, there are monthly premiums for these private Medicare supplemental policies. Most financial planners, myself included, think that you should seriously consider the comprehensive potential benefits of these policies that Medicare does not cover (or a Medicare Part C plan). As I stated earlier, this is not a part of my practice but there are many specialist Medigap insurance brokers who offer more than one insurer.

Medigap policies offered in most states are standardized and identified by letters A-N. Each policy letter (A-N) has its own benefits but each insurer must offer the same standard benefits for each policy. That allows consumers to compare apples to apples. Letter A is the most basic and least costly plan and the policy coverage benefits (and premiums) get more comprehensive from there with different letter plans.

So for example, every Medigap (A) policy in a state offers the same exact benefits. The only difference will be the financial strength of the insurer, their customer service and claims procedures... and the cost of the monthly premiums. The same would apply to Medigap (F) policy and so on.

Unlike most insurance policies, if you enroll during the 6 month open enrollment period that begins on the first day of the month that you are both age 65 and have Part B, there is no medical underwriting and you can buy whichever Medigap policy you want.

There are "usually" no pre-existing condition clauses or exclusions and you will pay the same as everyone else at that age for that particular letter policy.

However, don't miss that short window of time (once you are age 65 and have Part B) or you may find coverage difficult to find or very, very expensive to buy. Please note that if you are still covered by a group plan at work (with 20+ covered employees) the "clock" on your 6 months does NOT begin until you have enrolled in Part B - even if you are older than age 65.

If you do want to begin your benefits upon turning age 65, you would have to apply for Social Security three months beforehand. You should know that your eligibility does not begin until the first full month in which you are 65 for the complete month. So if you were born on June 10th, your first full month as a 65 year old would be July.

On a side note, future retirees should know that Medicare and Medigap plans will not pay for all of your medical expenses during your retirement. According to a study done by the Employee Benefit Research Institute, a 65 year old couple will spend an average of $283,000 out of their pockets over a 25 year retirement (excluding any long-term care costs). That works out to some $5,660 a year and does not include anticipated inflation.

The mutual fund giant, Fidelity does a similar study every year and comes up with a similar figure. Most of that enormous figure is for Medicare Part B, Part D and Medigap insurance premiums. The rest comes from non-covered expenses (co-pays, deductibles, etc.).

Ok, enough about Medicare (an area which is outside of my personal expertise). Let's move on.

How "Secure" is Social Security?

In a book about Social Security retirement benefits, I would be remiss if I didn't at least mention this topic.

The news about Social Security's prognosis for long-term viability has gotten progressively worse over the last number of years. Almost without exception, with every passing year, the Social Security Administration's own annual Trustees' Report has advanced the year when the Social Security Trust Funds are expected to run out of money and only depend on current inflows from workers to payout retiree benefits.

You can clearly see from the chart below how since just 2008, the Social Security Trust fund's estimate of the "run out of cash" date has already been accelerated by 7 years (from 2041 to 2034).

Trustee Report Year	Estimated "Out of Cash" Year
2015	2034
2014	2033 (unchanged from 2013)
2011	2036
2010	2037
2009	2037
2008	2041

Source: Social Security Administration.

Recent data published by the Congressional Budget Office (CBO) show that the Social Security Trust Funds' basic financial problems continue to get more worrisome. The combination of higher and longer disability claims, extremely low interest rates over the last 5 years, and growing life expectancies have all combined to speed up the year when the trust's reserves will be used-up. It's my personal opinion that the trust fund (without making vital changes asap) will run out even faster than what the CBO predicts.

If recent trends continue, the odds are pretty strong that the next Trustees' Report will put the trust funds' expiration date even sooner than the last report. And it is very likely that the pattern will keep on the same course if big changes are not made by Congress. So if nothing gets changed, and changed pretty quickly, the trusts past reserves will run out and retiree benefits will have to be cut.

According to the Social Security statement that we can all get online, the Social Security Trustees estimate that when the trust money is gone, incoming FICA taxes from current workers will only be able to cover about 79 percent of the program's promised benefits.

The average monthly Social Security check to a retiree is about $1,335 right now. While each retiree's situation is very different, a 21 percent cut in those benefits will be a substantial loss in income. Will that 21% reduction be evenly distributed amongst all beneficiaries? Or will other retirement income affect how much of a benefit reduction each retiree will get, such as low income retirees get no reduction while the "wealthy" lose more... or even all of their benefits.

The current projected year of the trust fund being exhausted is 2034. Depending upon when you are reading this book, that's just 20 years away. If you are a young retiree at age 65 now you will be age 85 then. That's about your life expectancy. But bear in mind that a couple aged 62 today has a joint life expectancy of age 92. That means there is a 50% chance that at least one of you will live 30 more years.

If that is the case, will you be able to survive during your final decade on a 25% loss of Social Security benefits? For many folks that would be a financial disaster.

Now it is almost impossible for me to fathom or believe that our ineffective Congress will continue to ignore the looming Social Security disaster. But the longer they delay making very simple, yet perhaps tough decisions, the more challenging the whole issue becomes.

Quite frankly, fixing Medicare and Medicaid are the REALLY tough issues to tackle and make fixing Social Security akin to a "cake walk".

There are many ways to fix the Social Security system and it will likely take a number of adjustments to the program to put the program on secure footing. This is not rocket science. It is simply a math problem. Although not easy for Congress to vote on, they need to make some decisions soon. To procrastinate is totally irresponsible.

If more money is going out than is coming in, then adjustments have to be made. An easy fix is to continue to delay the eligibility of benefits – both in extending early retirement from 62 to 65 over time as well as making full retirement age older (from age 66/67 to age 70 over time) for those 15 years or more from retirement now.

As life expectancies continue to rise, it makes no sense for all Americans to be "entitled" to have a longer retirement than their working career. Over a period of time, perhaps for those 50 or under now, the full retirement age might be raised and phased in over time from the current 67 (for those born in 1965 or later) to 70.

If the full retirement age (FRA) was increased to age 68 by the year 2028 it would reduce benefits by approximately 7 percent and eliminate 15 percent of Social Security's funding shortfall. If the full retirement age was increased to 70 by 2050 it would reduce benefits by about 21 percent and the deficit by a quarter.

However despite my personal beliefs, raising the Social Security retirement age is an unpopular idea, with only 37% of Americans supporting raising the retirement age to age 68, some 28% are in favor of increasing the full retirement age to 70.

One really quick way to fix the problem is to increase FICA taxes for either employees or both employers and employees. Employees currently pay 6.2 percent of their earnings into the Social Security system up to $118,500 in 2016. If that FICA tax rate was gradually increased to 7.2 percent by 2036, it would eliminate about half (53 percent) of Social Security's deficit. And if both employees and employers each paid the higher tax of 7.6 percent, it should totally eliminate the trust fund's financing gap.

As much as I hate paying higher taxes, I would guess that the amount of earned income that we all pay FICA taxes on (currently $118,500 in 2016) will be raised substantially. Individuals who earn more than this income threshold do not pay Social Security taxes on that excess income. There are bills in Congress to include all earned income (with no caps or limits) or up to something like $250,000.

According to the National Academy of Social Insurance (NASI), "if this tax cap was gradually eliminated between 2013 and 2022 it would reduce the deficit by 71 percent. And if the tax cap were increased over 5 years to include 90 percent of all earnings (currently about 84 percent of earnings are covered), this would reduce the financing gap by 30 percent. This tax cap change would affect the five percent of workers whose earnings exceed the cap, and they would receive somewhat higher benefits when they retire".

Another potential Social Security change is to reduce or eliminate Social Security benefits for people who have retirement incomes above a certain threshold. Billionaire investor Warren Buffet loves this idea and is personally lobbying for it. That's called "means testing". For example, if benefits were phased out for retirees with non-Social Security income between $55,000 and $110,000, the long term deficit would be reduced by 20 percent.

A recent survey by NASI found that 31% of Americans say they would like to means-test Social Security eligibility. It's interesting that many of those (69%) who would not even be financially affected by means testing do not like that idea much.

Certainly, there is quite a bit of fraud in the Social Security system, with a few dead people continually getting benefits. But the larger and most damaging fraud is done in the Social Security disability benefits area (profiled on 60 Minutes TV show). This is where working age folks claim a disability and get checks until they get caught, die or qualify for retiree benefits. This fraud is pervasive and costs taxpayers a small fortune -- although Social Security disability fraud pales in comparison to Medicaid and Medicare fraud which is much more pervasive.

At the moment, a proposal getting some serious consideration by President Obama is to tie the increases (COLA's) in Social Security payments to what is called "Chained CPI". This inflation "formula" simply slows the rate in which your benefits grow in response to inflation. If we switch to this COLA formula, it effectively is just a way to reduce benefits to both current _and_ future retirees. In other words, there would be less money going out to extend the trust funds.

President Obama's budget suggests that chained CPI could reduce the growth of the average Social Security check by some $30 a month in the next decade. If the chained CPI were used it would decrease the annual cost-of-living adjustment by an average of about 0.3 percentage points and reduce Social Security's deficit by 20 percent. Using the chained CPI would increase a $1,000 monthly benefit by just $27 instead of the $30 boost retirees would get using the current CPI formula. According to NASI, just 30% of Americans favor reducing the cost-of-living adjustment (proposal failed in 2014).

In my mind, a combination of some or all of the above fixes would put Social Security on secure footing. **But it is becoming much clearer to me that you can expect to be personally responsible to cover more of your retirement income needs through your own resources.** More of your retirement income will be up to you!

With the right financial advice you can better prepare for almost any eventuality. I would suggest that its makes prudent sense that you should prepare for a potential cut in benefits – whether via reductions in COLA's, means testing or higher taxes on future benefits.

Prudence would suggest that you hope for the best and prepare for the worst. How do you prepare? You do so by choosing the best Social Security strategy for your situation (a 21% potential cut in benefits on a smaller check can be much more detrimental than the same cut on a much larger monthly check). Additionally, you wisely invest your life savings to safely give you the most guaranteed income and asset protection along with "real" inflation growth to maintain the retirement lifestyle that you have dreamed about for decades.

How Secure is Your Pension from an Employer?

Speaking of preparing for the worst, do you or will you have an old-fashion pension from a previous employer? How secure is that income stream? Again, all of your retirement decisions should be taken in context of your overall circumstances.

While corporate pensions have been on the decline for many younger workers, a number of people nearing retirement still have pensions through their employers. But how secure is that pension? Do you have an option to take a lump sum or a "guaranteed" income stream for as long as you live? Are you confident that your employer will be able to keep its promise to you, despite its best intentions?

The Wilshire Consulting Group recently published a study that some 94% of corporate and municipal defined benefit plans (pensions) are "underfunded" and are in varying levels of distress of being able to fully deliver their promised benefits to current and future retirees. What does underfunded mean? It means that there have been larger promises made to current and future retirees than the pension has the funds to pay.

The Government Accountability Office (GAO) has continued to warn current and future retirees that the Pension Benefit Guaranty Corp.'s (PBGC) financial assistance to multi-employer plans continues to increase, threatening the financial solvency of the fund and therefore, its guarantees to retirees. Think of the PBGC as similar to what the FDIC is to banks – an added level of protection but with much less financial strength or power.

The Guarantee fund is supposed to cover and provide a minimum retirement income guarantee to more than 10 million workers and retirees. But since 2009, PBGC's financial assistance to the troubled retirement plans has increased dramatically, primarily because of a growing number of pension plan insolvencies. These plan insolvencies were caused by both very poor investment returns and too low levels of contributions to the pension plan from the employer.

By 2017, the PBGC expects the number of pension insolvencies to more than double, which will further stress the insurance fund. PBGC officials said that financial assistance to retirement pension plans that are insolvent or "are likely to become insolvent in the next 10 years" would likely exhaust the insurance fund within the next 10-15 years.

If the PBGC insurance fund is exhausted, many retirees will see their benefits reduced to an extremely small fraction of their original value because only a reduced stream of current insurance premium payments will be available to pay benefits to retirees.

According to MSN Money, nearly 80% of the private pension plans covered by the PBGC are underfunded by a total of some $740 billion. That's nearly three quarters of a TRILLION dollars' worth of promises made that are likely not to be fully kept.

The news is even worse among the nation's largest companies. It's hard to believe, but only 18 pension plans offered by companies that are part of the Standard & Poor's 500 are fully funded.

That works out to less than 4% of the biggest public companies in America that are financially ready to keep their full promises for their employee's retirement. That's pitiful.

According to the PBGC, over 1,400 companies shut down their pension plans in fiscal year 2011, compared with 1,200 in during 2009. An additional 152 pension plans failed (meaning they were terminated without enough money to pay promised benefits) and were taken over by the PBGC. Again the PBGC itself, which is funded by employer-paid insurance premiums, is running a $26 billion deficit. It is being held together by "duct tape" in the eyes of many people in-the-know.

I would be remiss to not mention government pension funds here as well. You probably already know that many local, county and state pension funds are in trouble. Right now, Detroit is in the news. Police, firefighters and teachers along with all of the other city employees are rightfully very worried about how secure the promises of a retirement (pension) are. We'll see what happens to them.

There are hundreds of towns, cities, counties and even a few states that have promised more than they will likely be able to deliver to both past and current employees. And the PBGC does not cover these types of pension funds.

According to a report by the State Budget Crisis Task Force, public pension funds (cities, towns, counties and states) are underfunded by at least $1 trillion. To begin to close that funding gap, 35 states have already reduced pension benefits for their employees, and half have dramatically increased worker contributions to their plans.

Three forward-thinking states -- Georgia, Michigan and Utah – and 1,000's of municipalities have implemented what is called "hybrid plans" that include defined contribution plans (which are similar to 401k's), that shift some investment risk to workers. Expect more and more public pension funds to follow that lead each year.

Even fully funded retirement plans aren't exempt from big changes. General Motors (GM), was once considered the "role model" for running a solid retiree plan. But it shocked its salaried retirees by announcing it was passing-off their pension obligations to Prudential Financial. Over 40,000 GM retirees had to make the difficult decision of whether to take a lump-sum settlement from GM then or trust Prudential to send them monthly checks for the rest of their lives.

The bottom line is that even though you are "counting" on a company or government pension (or even a company/government retirement health plan) in the years to come, you might consider figuring out how secure that "promise" will be (and a promise is all that it really is). Any pension plan or health plan can be frozen, shut down or altered, changing how much you can expect in retirement.

To find out how underfunded your own pension is, simply request that information from your HR department and carefully READ and review the annual benefit and funding statements that your plan is required to provide every year - so you can gauge its health. Anything below 80% funding is cause for concern and perhaps a very good reason to seriously look at taking a lump sum (and run!) if it's offered.

Taking a lump sum has its pros and cons (like everything else in this world). You can control the investment and perhaps enjoy a much higher income and have potential inflation protection (most pension income amounts are fixed for your life). Or you could take the lump sum and then buy a guaranteed annuity income stream from an insurance company which is likely in much better financial shape than your employer. Again, everyone's situation is different and you should seek advice from a highly qualified and experienced financial advisor.

One topic that often comes up with married clients is the question of a "survivor" option that is often made available to pensioners: should you take a single life option and collect the highest monthly payout (but only until you die), or take a lesser income and ensure that 100% or some lower percentage of your benefit would go to your spouse if something were to happen to you?

A potential solution to this question is for you to consider something called "pension maximization". The idea that we are trying to address then is: Can you buy life insurance to replace the pension for less than the monthly "cost or reduction of income" of taking the survivor option? How exactly does pension maximization work?

Here is a just one example where one client could take a single life pension of $4,000/month or choose a 100% survivor option for 3,400/month (so the spouse will continue to get the income after the pensioners death). That survivor's option then "costs" $600/month ($4,000 – $3,400) in lower monthly income. When considering a potential life insurance option, we would need to replace this income stream based on the pensioner's passing away in year one with the following policies.

Of course, life insurance costs vary greatly and depend upon the age, health, lifestyle and the type of policy one chooses and the insurer. But here is a sample of costs using the layering approach:

A 10 year term policy for $225,000 ($45/month)

A 15 year term policy for $125,000 ($33/month)

A 20 year term policy for $100,000 ($32/month)

A 25 year term policy for $105,000 ($55/month)

A 30 year term policy for $110,000 ($106/month)

A guaranteed never-to-lapse universal life policy for $275,000 ($275/month)

There are multiple ways to handle this pension income replacement strategy with life insurance. This is just one of them.

You could get a number of different term policies and a "lifetime" policy which give you more life insurance in the early years (at a lower cost than one big "never-lapse" policy) and less coverage down the road as life expectancy dwindles. This is shown above. The reason you might "layer" different term life insurance policies as in the above example is because your spouse needs less insurance as you get older since the time you need the insurance death benefit to last (income replacement) is shorter.

If you add up the above policies, you get a monthly expense of $546/month. That costs $54/month less than the "cost" of the 100% joint survivor option (your income would be $600 lower than if the pension only lasted for one lifetime). After 10 years, the $45/month policy drops. So in effect, you would get a raise of $45/month then. By the time the 20 year policy has lapsed, you'd save almost $1,300 more per year than when you started.

As an added benefit, if the spouse dies before the pensioner, then one could cancel the all of the insurance and save the premiums or keep some of the insurance to pass on to their heirs.

Who might this strategy work well for? People who have kids or family they want to leave money to. If both spouses passed way together early on, their heirs would receive no additional money under the pension and survivor options. But by using a pension maximization strategy as described above, this couple's kids or grandkids could receive as much as $940,000 income tax free. With the pension-only option, the kids get no benefit from your pension whatsoever. A pension can only pass to a spouse – not to kids.

Again, would pension maximization work well for you? Maybe, maybe not. Sometimes, the company pension option is the best choice and you don't have to go through any medical underwriting. Like everything else in life, there are pros and cons to each side. Very seldom is an important decision like this, a black and white one.

The 3 Buckets of Risk and the 3 Buckets of Taxation

At the beginning of this book, I described Social Security as a very important stream of retirement income for the vast majority of Americans. For millions of retirees every year, making the right filing decision based on their life and financial circumstances and goals is of paramount importance. Barring something very crazy (and if this is the case all bets are probably off in every area of your financial life too), for all but the very wealthy (as determined by Congress), your checks from Social Security are guaranteed for life regardless of the economy. They will come in like clockwork every single month for as long as you or your spouse live, and with some type of COLA's the checks will very likely grow substantially over your full retirement.

So these guaranteed checks will form the base retirement income for most retirees. But as stated earlier in the book, Social Security checks will not provide everything one needs to pay the bills. For many retirees, income from a part or full time job will be necessary as they have no or little savings to provide for a meaningful supplemental income stream. This next section will be of no practical value to these people who for whatever reason, have no savings or investments to speak of. But for those readers who do have savings in IRA's, old 401(k)'s, 403(b)'s, CD's, brokerage accounts, etc., I think you will really find the next few pages of great interest.

Let me ask you? When your portfolio crashed in 2000-2002 and again in 2008, did your financial advisor tell you not to worry – "just hang in there -- that it's only a loss on paper"? Or did you convince yourself of that nonsense if you manage your money yourself? How did you feel when you opened those awful monthly or quarterly statements? The newest statement was even worse than the last one!

Well if that is true, then did your advisor tell you that your gains in 2003-2007 and again in 2009-2014 that your gains are only "paper" ones and not to feel good about them? No, he/she basked in the glory.

Those past losses were very real. And if you are going to be using your savings to help fund your retirement lifestyle by taking a monthly income from them over the next 20, 30 or 40 years, can you afford to participate in the next major market downturn? If your accounts drop by 15%, 20% or more, can (or should) you still take the same monthly withdrawal as before without jeopardizing your outliving your money?

It is widely known and believed in the community of Certified Financial Planners™, that the "distribution" phase (taking income) is VERY different than the "accumulation" phase (saving for retirement). However, it has been my experience, based on years of reviewing actual portfolio's, whether managed by the individual or by an advisor, that they are not treated differently... as they absolutely should be.

In my fee-based investment management practice in Atlanta, I so clearly remember a number of couples that I spoke with during 1998 and 1999 who were BellSouth, Nortel, Lucent and Home Depot employees (among many other companies as well). These "prospective clients" were going to retire "early and rich" based on the values of their company stocks and 401K portfolios. Most of these folks had already decided to retire – and give up their 6-figure jobs before age 60 and planned on taking 5%, 6% or even 7% income distributions (plus COLA's for inflation) from their accounts that had grown by 20%-30% or more a year in the late 1990's.

Then 2000 came. Then 2001 and 2002 followed. That changed everything for these people. Their accounts had fallen by 30%-50% on top of the hefty monthly cash withdrawals taken out to solely fund their retirement lifestyles. It wasn't pretty. It wasn't pretty at all.

During the accumulation phase (up to a few years before retirement) people can afford to take more risk as they have more time to recover. However, like the couples just described, the distribution phase is very different. Taking withdrawals during a bad bear market can dramatically upset and forever alter the longevity of a planned retirement lifestyle... and your continued peace of mind.

So when I meet a prospective new client on the phone, internet or in person, one of the first things that I like to do is talk about the 3 buckets of risk. More specifically, I call it the 3 buckets of risk and return, but my clients just like to call it the 3 buckets of risk.

This is a very simple and easy-to-understand way for my clients to clearly decide for themselves, how much risk they can live with and sleep at night during their retirement (distribution phase). What I have them decide is how much of their investable assets as a percentage (excluding their home) would they like to have invested in each of 3 risk/return buckets: 1) the Safe and Secure bucket, 2) the Moderate Risk bucket and 3) the High Risk bucket. You can see the 3 buckets below as well as a brief summary of the bucket's risk/return profile.

SAFE and SECURE

Absolutely NO CHANCE of LOSS
of Principal

Looking for Annual Returns of
3%-5%
Over the Next 3-5 Years

I want _____ **%**
of my savings in this bucket

MODERATE RISK

Loss of Principal
Generally Limited to 4%-5%
in a Year in the Bad Years

Looking for Annual Returns of
6%-7%... Maybe 8%
Over the Next 5, 10 or 15 Years

I want _____ **%**
of my savings in this bucket

HIGH RISK

Loss of Principal
Generally Limited to 10%-15% in a Year...
But Can Lose Up To 50%
or More in the Worst of Times

Looking for Annual Returns of 9%-10% or
More Over the Next 5, 10 or 15 Years --
After the Full Roller Coaster Ride

I want _____ **%**
of my savings in this bucket

Let's expand a bit on each of the brief descriptions inside of each bucket. The **Safe and Secure bucket** is exactly as it says. This is money that will never go down in value. Many people think of CD's and 90-day Treasury bills here, and in normal times they might provide an expected return of 3%-5% --- but certainly not over the last 6-7 years. CD's and T-bills have paid less than 1% over the last few years. And it is very important to understand (especially with extremely low CD rates now) that if that "safe" money is not earning an after-tax return equal to inflation, (CD's right now) your principal is losing purchasing power. So in this sense there could be a "real loss" -- but no losses are ever shown on your monthly, quarterly or annual account statements.

But the safe assets I use can safely and consistently provide 3%-5% without any risk to principal. In baseball terms, these investments are just like walks – you have no risk of getting "thrown out" on your way to first base. There is no volatility and you never go backwards.

The **Moderate Risk bucket** (multi-asset fixed income) is for people who want or need a higher return... and are willing to take some predictable and reasonable risks in order to earn bigger returns over time. With the 33 year-long bull market in BONDS ending, they alone are not a good "buy and hold" now. It's possible, although not typical for this diversified bucket to lose a small percentage of your principal in a bad year, but this bucket can be pretty dependable over time.

The investments in this bucket generally provide average annual returns of 6%-7% over a period of 5, 10 or 15 years with some mild fluctuations (volatility) in value. During the worst of times in 2008-2009 this portfolio-type lost no more than 4%-5% before rebounding.

The **High Risk bucket** is exactly what it's named. Most savers invest in stocks, mutual funds, ETF's, variable annuities, IPO's, private placements, hedge funds, limited partnerships, etc. to earn high returns (9%-10% or more) to compensate for much higher risk than either of the other two buckets. The High Risk bucket is better suited for "accumulation over time" than for monthly retirement income.

Over time, you might get 9%-10% or higher returns -- although the S&P 500 returned virtually nothing during the period of 2000-2011. That's a dozen years with nearly 0% returns (excluding 2%-2.5% dividends). All with tremendous volatility (with large and scary losses) along the way. In fact, including dividends from 2000-20015 the total annualized return of the S&P 500 was only about 5%. Taking income from volatile investments is not a good thing. Again in baseball terms, this is trying to hit homeruns (with many strikeouts along the way).

During 2000-2002 the market dropped by about -40%. In calendar year 2008 the market (S&P 500 index) fell some -37% -- however from peak to trough in 2008 to March 2009, the index actually fell by -51%.

Even during 2011, a year in which the S&P 500 index price began at 1258 and ended the year at the same price of 1258 (but earning some 2.1% in dividends that year), there was huge volatility – price swings. In this calendar year alone, there were 13 periods when the price of the index went up or down by 7% or more! Thirteen times! That is a lot of volatility to withstand to only earn 2.1% of dividends – especially while drawing a monthly income.

When you are in the accumulation phase, you have time to recover from (ride out) these market drops. However, many people panic and sell near the bottom, only to buy back in again near the top once they begin to forget the earlier financial pain. But when you are taking distributions that is completely another thing altogether.

So the first thing my new clients do is tell me how much of their assets (as a percentage) do they want in each risk bucket. How much to allow them to sleep at night... no matter what is going on in the economy or the markets. There is no right or wrong answer. The only answer that matters is the one that gives you peace of mind and helps you attain your goals. Oftentimes, the husband has one set of percentages in mind while the wife has a different set that she feels most comfortable with (usually more conservative). Then it's just a matter of making a compromise that they both can easily live with.

Getting the right mix (for YOU) of percentages of your assets in the right bucket is the first step in the investment process. This is an easy step for you to complete - just go with your gut feeling on what you would feel comfortable with -- no matter what is happening now, or can or will happen in the future in the stock, bond, real estate or commodities markets. But here is the strange part.

Most people's "desired" percentages in their risk buckets... are NOTHING like how their portfolios are actually invested. It's crazy.

When I do portfolio reviews for new potential clients, I find that nearly 90% of the time, the percentages they say they WANT in each of their 3 buckets... is absolutely nowhere near what they actually HAVE. It's hardly ever even close! Either their current financial advisor isn't asking the right questions or isn't paying much, if any, attention to your answers and feelings. This is a recipe for emotional pain.

The next step in the process is to find the lowest risk (lowest volatility) investments for the two "non-safe and secure" buckets to provide the expected returns over time to attain your goals. That's where a professional can add great value and experience (as well as provide access to special guaranteed income investments). This way, the investor's aversion to overall risk and financial returns will be better combined to reach their retirement objectives... and sleep at night. It doesn't have to be difficult to attain your goals. If you could get the same investment return with lower risk, wouldn't you do so?

Again, the question is how much of your investable assets should be invested in each bucket to help you reach your financial goals... while allowing you to sleep at night in virtually any market conditions? Sometimes one must take on a bit more risk to reach their income or savings goals at the expense of their complete peace of mind – in order to "catch up" or "make-up" for a low past savings rate... or to overcome a history of poor investing. But investors should carefully consider taking much more risk than they need to in order to attain their financial goals and objectives. If you can't live with it – don't try.

Your risk/reward preferences (bucket allocation) will likely change over time and your choices of investments should then mirror those changes. Take a few minutes and write down how you would allocate your buckets? If you have a spouse, each of you do this and compare.

In my practice, I prefer to use special investments for the Safe and Secure bucket that will likely enjoy average annual returns of 3%-5% (over the next 4-6 years) with no risk to principal (as described earlier). Especially ones that guarantee a lifetime income that grows over time.

In the Moderate Risk bucket, I like to use unique investments that have long track records (15-20 years) of never having a losing calendar year (although that is in no way a guarantee of the future). However there have been a number of quarters over those years with small losses of 1%-3%. Clients with money in this bucket know about and accept these reasonable risks – especially when they have a good percentage of their other investments in the Safe and Secure bucket.

And for the percentage of assets that most of my retired clients put in their High Risk bucket, I use investments that historically have "50% or less" of the volatility of the stock market (the S&P 500 index) BUT have similar long-term returns. Why take more risk than you need to in order for that portion of your portfolio to do very well?

The goal in retirement income planning is to <u>maximize</u> the income while <u>minimizing</u> the risks and volatility of your investments. I like to use a low-risk portfolio (with the least likely amount of volatility) in order to have monthly income stability and a high probability of long-term retirement success (not outliving your money). Less stress! That's opposed to most portfolios that I see, that are what I call a "hope and a prayer" portfolio -- stuffed with high risk, highly volatile mutual funds, stocks, real estate, commodities and even "bad" bonds.

There have been 9 recessions and bear markets since 1957 (the year I was born). That works out to one about every 6.33 years on average. We had 2000-2002. The last one was in 2008-2009. As of this revised edition in December 2015, we're 6.5 years from the last one.

Is the next one going to be in 2016, 2017 or 2018… and how bad will it be? Whenever the next one is, I can tell you one thing. If you and/or your spouse are going to live some 20-30 years or more in retirement, you will likely experience another 4 to 6 of these bear markets and recessions (along with periods of very low interest rates again). Are you fully financially and emotionally prepared for this?

Have you spent most of the first decade of this new century, just recouping the past gains you had earned before the market dropped yet once again in 2008/2009? Taking 2 steps forward, one step back (over and over again)? I hate taking unnecessary investment losses more than I do paying income taxes!

As I write this book, U.S. stock markets are at near all-time highs (new highs in 2015). With that said, the founder of Vanguard Funds, John Bogle, has stated twice during interviews on CNBC TV (2014) and elsewhere that he expects two bad bear markets with stocks dropping up to 50% in the next 10 years or so. What if he's only half right?

Will the portfolio that you currently have, safely weather any of these steep market drops and continue to provide the same (and inflation protected) income to supplement your guaranteed Social Security checks? Social Security is your base, but what about the rest?

I won't go into which unique investments I use for each bucket as that is beyond the scope of this book. But it is imperative that most of my readers understand what allocations of investments they want to go into each bucket so they can sleep at night – while providing a safe monthly investment income to supplement their Social Security checks. To me, that is the only definition of a good portfolio – one that safely provides the needed investment income while letting you sleep at night – no matter what's happening in the economy.

Would you like to see how closely your desired percentages in your 3 buckets… actually match your current portfolio? You will likely be very surprised… and sometimes even very upset with your current advisor or even your own portfolio choices. Better to know the truth.

There is no cost or obligation for me to help you with this. Simply call or email me for a fully independent and 100% verifiable, objective review of your existing portfolio and learn how it's already allocated.

Now like the 3 buckets of risk, I also like to teach my clients about the 3 tax buckets. As we saw earlier in the book with the Earlys, the Waites and the Bests, keeping your income taxes as low as possible is another important part of your retirement income plan. You have probably heard about these 3 buckets before, but have you actually tried to put the "right" investments into the "right" tax buckets? It can make a big financial difference over 2-3 decades of your retirement.

There are **3 basic types of tax buckets** to hold investments or money in: 1) Taxable 2) Tax-Deferred and 3) Tax-Free. Given the choice, most folks would choose to keep the majority of their assets in the **tax-free bucket** for obvious reasons. When I begin working with a client in their 30's, 40's and 50's, this is pretty easy to do. But it is often much harder near or during retirement. There are only three kinds of investments that offer tax-free characteristics: ROTH IRA's, muni-bonds and cash-value life insurance. Few people I meet with have very much in this tax bucket before they work with me.

For many people, the **tax-deferred bucket** is the next best thing. You "postpone" the tax. Tax-deferred buckets are traditional IRA's, 401(k)'s, 403(b)'s, and other "qualified" accounts as well as annuities. When you hold money in tax-deferred investments you have much more control of when you get taxed (upon taking withdrawals). Unlike non-qualified annuities, qualified money such as traditional IRA's have to be slowly withdrawn (and fully taxed) at age 70½. These forced withdrawals are called Required Minimum Distributions (RMDs).

For many of my clients who do not need to take the mandatory RMD's to maintain their lifestyle, this is a big thorn in their side and can sometimes even push them into a higher tax-bracket. And as you saw with the Waites and the Bests it can even cause more of your Social Security checks to become taxable.

Taxable investments are those in which you get a 1099, K-1 or a similar form every year which notifies the I.R.S. that you earned interest, dividends, short or long term capital gains – whether you withdrew the gains... or not! You must pay the taxes each year you have interest or gains. Even if your account is lower at the end of the year than it was at the beginning... the tax-man (I.R.S.) wants his share.

Most people that I see have the majority of their funds in the taxable and tax-deferred buckets and the least amount in the tax-free. Most folks quickly understand the benefits of making some smart money moves to reduce current taxes and increase spendable income.

And as you read earlier, where you keep your money can affect how much of your Social Security checks get taxed... and sometimes at what tax rate. If you can reduce your taxes, you can spend more money and enjoy a better lifestyle on the same gross income. The two slides below show what I typically see in prospective client portfolios (left slide) and more like what I'd rather them have (the right slide).

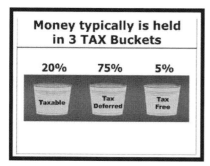 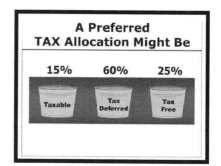

For most people there are simple money moves to get more of your funds in the best tax buckets for you and cut your tax bill. When you combine designing an investment portfolio and supplemental income stream by using the 3 buckets of risk along with wisely using the 3 tax buckets, you can truly transform your retirement years. You can dramatically slash your investment risk, enjoy more peace of mind and even cut your annual "contributions" to the I.R.S. Making the "right" money moves is up to you. But it can make a real difference.

Putting Retirement ALL Together

As stated numerous times in this book, I believe the decision on how and when to file for Social Security should never be made on a standalone basis. Such a critical decision should be based on your entire financial situation and goals – taking into account your anticipated retirement lifestyle expenses, likely longevity (of both spouses), any pensions and all assets, as well as your tolerance for risk.

One of the most important services I offer my clients is to design a <u>written</u> lifetime retirement income plan. A plan that details exactly where (from Social Security, pensions, investments, etc.) the income will come from to give them the <u>rising</u> monthly income they desire for the rest of their life or lives. Most pre-retirees and retirees do not have a written plan or sound lifetime retirement income roadmap. Most folks describe the path they are on as mostly "just winging it". I can tell after our first discussion whether or not your current income plan (assuming you even have one) is going to blow-up on you and cause some dramatically adverse changes in your ongoing lifestyle.

Do you want a real retirement income plan with a high probability of long-term success or something where you're likely going to have to substantially reduce your retirement lifestyle when you are 75 or 80?

Many clients describe the written income plan I designed for them as a "business plan for retirement". It gives them a year-by-year timeline of what account they will be withdrawing "X" amount of dollars from and why, to fund their desired lifestyle. You'll understand exactly what we're doing and exactly why we're going to do it. And like any business plan, we review it annually and make adjustments.

That retirement income plan maximizes your <u>after-tax spendable</u> income, capital preservation and reduces the risk and volatility in your portfolio. It's one that will take you through age 100+ with as much predictable and reliable income as possible. Contact me to learn more.

Final Thoughts of Filing for Social Security

It is my sincere hope that the title of my book, "Social Security Income Planning: The Baby Boomers' Guide to Maximize Your Retirement Benefits" has fully lived up to its name for you. I had originally envisioned the final section of this book to be frequently asked questions and answers... but the more I thought about it, the less helpful I believed it would be.

The thing I hate the most about TV and radio financial shows is that callers call in and are given 30 seconds to explain their situation and ask their question. And nine times out of ten, the host "expert" doesn't even ask any follow-up questions or get more clarification before they "throw-up" an answer. And then on to the next caller. And the same could be said for newspaper columns and so on.

Now I understand that these shows are for "entertainment" purposes only, as most of these "experts" have no training, experience or professional credentials to be the ultimate source for answers for every single question. But I doubt that most of the callers (and the full audience) understand this and take the 1 minute "answer" as gospel.

And after much thought, I certainly did not want to do the same thing to my readers – give answers to questions without knowing the full financial situation (and other non-financial circumstances).

Having said that, I invite my readers to contact me directly if they believe I might add significant value to their retirement planning. I will take more than a few minutes to listen and fully understand your situation before I even think about offering a response. There is no cost, nor any obligation to have a 15-20 minute phone conversation with me. And if you'd like, I can also show you examples of my written retirement income plans. Please be patient if I'm traveling and not available within 24-48 hours. But I will not forget about you or leave you hanging. I promise you that it will definitely be worth the wait!

About the Author: Mark J. Orr, CFP®

770-777-8309 Office
mark@SmartFinancialPlanning.com

www.SmartFinancialPlanning.com
2050 Marconi Drive Suite #300   Alpharetta, GA 30005

Mark has been a practicing Certified Financial Planner since 2000. Certified Financial Planners are held to the strictest ethical and fiduciary standards and must study for two years prior to taking a 10 hour long exam that less than 60% of test takers pass the first time. Since 1997, he has held life, health and the Series 7 Securities license and became a Registered Investment Advisor representative soon thereafter. In July 2012, he happily gave up his stockbroker's license since he felt that it was in direct conflict with his registered investment advisory business and his core beliefs as being a fiduciary to his clients – always putting their interests above his own.

He actually began his financial services career as a Long Term Care Insurance Specialist in 1997 and has since greatly expanded his practice to better serve his clients throughout the USA. In 1998, he opened up his own fee-only Registered Investment Advisory business, MORR Capital Management, Inc.

Through this firm, he manages his clients' investments – primarily using proven low-risk, low-volatility private wealth money managers. These accounts are allocated into low-volatility portfolios based on a client's tolerance for risk (the "Moderate Risk" and "Higher Risk" buckets), time horizon, tax situation, as well as their monthly income and legacy goals.

A second specialty (the safe and secure bucket) is using a few very unique tax-deferred income annuities to <u>guarantee</u> a lifetime income (for both spouses). That monthly income has great potential to grow every single year. All without taking any stock market risk <u>and</u> without giving up access to your cash. They can be very powerful additions to Social Security income – since both checks are guaranteed for life and have potential inflation protection.

Another main focus of his financial practice is using cash value life insurance for tax-free retirement income (a very attractive alternative to a ROTH IRA with many living-benefits). His books, "Stress-Free Retirement Planning" and "Recession-Proof Retirement" fully discuss these policies and much more.

He is the author of several white papers and ebooks and has led dozens of public seminars on various financial planning topics. He's been quoted in the USA TODAY as well as being a guest on several morning radio shows across the country. Prior to the financial services business, Mark spent the early part of his career in the luxury resort real estate marketing and development industry – managing $100 million of sales in Europe over a 7 year period.

He is a two-time past board member of his local Rotary Club and continues to be active in community service through the Rotary Club and other community affairs. On a personal note, Mark and Norma live in Alpharetta, Georgia and love to travel – especially to warm sandy beaches in the sun. Staying in good shape is important to him and he enjoys good red wine. Finally, he is the very proud father of three grown children (Megan, Marina and Michael) and three wonderful grandchildren.

CFP

**Thank you again for your purchase and for reading my book.
I hope that it has opened your eyes to the many wonderful
possibilities ahead for you during your retirement!**

Made in the USA
San Bernardino, CA
26 December 2016